INDIA: *Emergent Power?*

National Strategy Information Center
Board of Editors

Frank N. Trager, Chairman
Frank R. Barnett
Dorothy E. Nicolosi
Joyce E. Larson

INDIA:
Emergent Power?

Stephen P. Cohen
and
Richard L. Park

Published by
Crane, Russak &
Company, Inc.
New York

National Strategy
Information Center, Inc.

India: Emergent Power?

Published in the United States by
Crane, Russak & Company, Inc.
347 Madison Avenue
New York, N.Y. 10017

© 1978 by National Strategy Information Center, Inc.
111 East 58th Street
New York, N.Y. 10022

No part of this publication may be reproduced,
stored in a retrieval system, or transmitted
in any form or by any means, electronic,
mechanical photocopying, recording,
or otherwise, without the prior
written permission of the publisher.

Library Edition: ISBN: 0-8448-1351-6
Paperbound Edition: ISBN: 0-8448-1353-2
LC 78-50920

Strategy Paper No. 33

Printed in the United States of America

Contents

Preface	VII
AUTHORS' INTRODUCTION *The Carter Administration and India*	XIII
CHAPTER 1 *India's Status As A World Power*	1
CHAPTER 2 *Analytical Perspectives*	9
CHAPTER 3 *India's Nuclear Potential*	43
CHAPTER 4 *Strategic Implications for the United States*	54
CHAPTER 5 *General Conclusions*	71
APPENDICES AND BIBLIOGRAPHICAL NOTE	
Appendix A: India in Comparative Perspective	77
Appendix B: Indian Defense Production	80
Appendix C: Weapons and Force Inventory	84
Bibliographical Note	87

Preface

India has long been linked to "Gandhism," pacifism, and nonviolence in the minds of many foreign observers. Professors Stephen P. Cohen and Richard L. Park, the authors of this careful study of India's strategic policies and capabilities, make clear, however, that defense and military concerns play a critical role in shaping India's relations with its neighbors and with outside powers. Moreover, despite its poverty, it is clear that India has substantial military-industrial assets and a growing nuclear potential that enhance its geopolitical importance.

India's 1974 "peaceful" nuclear explosion dramatically raised the question of national and regional security in the subcontinent to the level of international concern and demonstrated that India may soon become a factor in world politics. India's role as a major regional power lends weight to its role as an intermediary in the North-South dialogue; and "more than ever before," the authors argue, "India is exhibiting its independence abroad, backed by a large and improving military force, and a growing, advanced industrial economy, within the framework of political stability." Since 1971, India has increased the size of its frigate, destroyer, and submarine fleet, and India may be expected to play a small but significant role in the Persian Gulf and Indian Ocean—areas which have gained in strategic importance along with the increased European, Japanese, and American dependence upon Persian Gulf oil.

Professors Cohen and Park show that India's serious problems of economic development, population growth, and widespread poverty have not prevented the building of a large, modernized defense force, supported by industrial development, centers for the training of scientific and technological elites, and the rapid expansion of a management group capable of handling the complexities of leadership for an emergent power. The rapid expansion of India's defense production base, greatly strengthened since India's 1962 conflict with China, reflects India's successful combination of the material resources, technology, and organizational skills of the "modern advanced sector" with enormous manpower resources available at relatively low cost.

In stressing the growth of India's international influence the authors do not forget the fact that Indo-American relations have for decades been characterized by tensions over issues in both regional and global affairs that are often based on serious differences in perception and interest. India has strongly resented, for example, United States military and political ties with Pakistan, for long an important and loyal US ally. Americans have been troubled by India's refusal to sign the Non-Proliferation Treaty, the long-standing left-socialist inclinations of some of India's leaders, India's voting patterns in the United Nations, and the country's "tilt" toward the Soviet Union formalized in the 1971 Indo-Soviet Treaty of Peace, Friendship and Cooperation.

There is reason to hope, however, that the election of Prime Minister Morarji Desai may have set the stage for warmer relationships between the United States and India. Despite indications that the Desai government will continue amicable Indo-Soviet relations, the Moscow connection is not likely to inhibit the development of India's other world ties. India's leverage in regional and world politics, stress Cohen and Park, makes imperative the renewal of dialogue between the United States and India on a number of crucial and conflict-laden issues, such as the development of nuclear energy, weapons proliferation, and the future organization of the international economic order.

The authors argue that the US recognition of India's regional hegemony need not imply the abandonment of equally legitimate American interests in, for example, the stability and security of Pakistan, nor is it to be expected that Indian and American viewpoints and objectives will always overlap. Yet if the world's two largest democracies can transcend the resentments, moralizing, and ideological hostility of the recent past, more cooperative relations between the US and India will contribute to the aim of political and economic stability in the South Asia area.

Stephen P. Cohen was educated at the Universities of Chicago and Wisconsin, and since 1965 has held a joint appointment in the Department of Political Science and the Center for Asian Studies at the University of Illinois, Urbana. Professor Cohen is the author of *The Indian Army* and numerous articles and monographs on South Asian foreign and defense policies. He presently is completing a study of regional arms control and disarmament problems under the auspices of The Ford Foundation.

Richard L. Park has been involved in studies of India for

over thirty years, and has written widely on the subcontinent's domestic and foreign policies. He was educated at Northwestern and Harvard Universities; taught at the University of California, Berkeley; was Dean of Social Sciences at the University of Pittsburgh; and presently is Professor of Political Science and Associate of the Center for South and Southeast Asian Studies at the University of Michigan. Professor Park is President of The Association for Asian Studies (1978-1979). A revised edition of his *India's Political System* (with Bruce Bueno de Mesquita) will appear in 1978.

Frank R. Barnett, *President*
National Strategy Information Center, Inc.

June 1978

Authors' Introduction

The Carter Administration and India:
A REVIEW OF THE FIRST EIGHTEEN MONTHS

It may come as a surprise to readers of this study to realize that military defense, aspirations for regional and global influence, leadership in the building of a new international economic order, and the gradual curtailment of superpower dominance over world affairs have been central policies of the Government of India since its founding in 1947. Certainly themes of this order did not constitute the core of President Jimmy Carter's public speeches in New Delhi during his stay there in January 1978, nor upon his return to Washington, and have not since. The critical role of defense policy in shaping India's relations with its neighbors, as well as with the super, great, and middle powers, has not had the same sharp focus for observers abroad that economic and political development have had. Nonetheless, India has moved slowly but steadily toward its role as a regional great power. More than ever before, India is exhibiting its independence abroad, backed by a large and improving military force, and a growing, advanced industrial economy, within the framework of political stability.

India no longer can be treated merely as a large pawn in even larger scaled world power strategies. Foreign gov-

XIV · THE CARTER ADMINISTRATION AND INDIA

ernmental participants in relations with India have not been innocent of these power-related interests in South Asia, but many of our politicians, journalists, and certainly the general public show little sophisticated understanding of current realities in that region of Asia. Few abroad, including the United States, take India seriously as a world power, and this is a regrettable mistake. If one adopts the perspectives of twenty-five years hence, India looms large as a crucial factor.

I

When President Carter took office early in 1977, India was at its low point politically, under the authoritarian Emergency regime mounted by Prime Minister Indira Gandhi on June 26, 1975. Most of the opposition leaders (and some from her own party) were in jail; upwards of 100,000 citizens ultimately were imprisoned; the press was censored so rigorously that even the government was uninformed about conditions in the country; Sanjay Gandhi, Mrs. Gandhi's son, behaved like a *goonda* (thug); the courts were shackled by draconian limitations on their normal constitutional powers, limits approved by a pliable and irresponsible Parliament; enforced sterilization policies to limit population growth led to extreme excesses by cowed or brutalized administrative officers; and trade unions were locked into pay and work policies without access to grievance procedures. Economically, there were some advances under more orderly if toughly policed conditions, but the advantages were given to the well-off, rather than to the down-and-out. Despite the forthright and courageous resistance of many who believed in an open political society, it appeared that India was damned to a long seige of suffering under Indira Gandhi's strong, ubiquitous political hand.

Because of her own party's pressure for political security, and with an eye to the legitimization of the Emergency, Mrs. Gandhi called a parliamentary election in March 1977. The results were not what she had expected. She herself was defeated in her own constituency, and her party was swept from power by a loosely-knit coalition called the Janata (People's) Party, under the national leadership of Jayaprakash Narayan and Morarji Desai—a group not even formed as an established party until May 1, 1977. The Janata Party's impressive victory was enhanced by the defection of a senior Cabinet minister, Jagjivan Ram, at the last moment before the election. (Later, in June 1977 and in the winter of 1978, elections in the states confirmed the Janata Party's national strength, although Mrs. Gandhi made some progress in a political comeback by victories in certain south Indian states.)

Morarji Desai, a conservative, octagenarian ex-Congress Party leader, and an arch political foe of Mrs. Gandhi for a number of years, took over the prime ministership and formed a government from his ex-opposition followers, who ranged from the democratic socialist left to a highly conservative right.

The election was fought not so much over specific issues as over "democracy" (Janata Party) versus "authoritarianism" (Congress Party). Tens of millions of illiterate peasants and workers had their say, and what they said favored an open political system. The Emergency and the general election of 1977 were momentous events in world history, although few analysts have yet realized that the 1975–1977 period in India was a test of democracy fully the equivalent in significance of a social revolution.

XVI · THE CARTER ADMINISTRATION AND INDIA

II

The stage was prepared for a fresh set of relationships between India and the United States. Morarji Desai, a former Deputy Prime Minister and Finance Minister, was experienced in dealing with the United States. He had not approved of the imbalance created by close relations with the USSR developed by the Congress Party over the years since the mid-1960s. President Carter possessed little knowledge about India, but his mother had been there with the Peace Corps in the 1960s, and the President's moral and religious inclinations were affected by the concept of nonviolent resistance to wrongs, well known to him through the writings of Mahatma Gandhi. Moreover, the plight of India's poor had a grip on him personally, and he seemed determined to make human rights, including the right to a decent life, a strong plank in his foreign policy.

There followed an extensive private correspondence between the new Prime Minister and the new President that continues, as well as an exchange of ambassadors, each carrying in his person symbols of the desire for rapprochement. Robert F. Goheen, former President of Princeton and himself born in India, was sent to New Delhi; somewhat later, Nani A. Palkhivala, one of India's leading lawyers, and an articulate spokesman for democracy, the rule of law, and free enterprise, was sent to Washington. Andrei Gromyko, Foreign Minister of the USSR, came to India in April 1977, and Morarji Desai went to Moscow in October of the same year, with results that assured the continuation of amicable Indo-Soviet relations, but on a more even level in relationship to other world ties. To restore India's nonalignment policy to "tiltless" condition, it was Morarji Desai's policy to strengthen

U.S. and British accords, among others, and to lessen those with the USSR. The People's Republic of China and Pakistan also are receiving special consideration as conditions permit.

III

In concrete terms, much less than might have been expected has developed so far in improving Indo-American relations. Some $60 million in foreign aid has been earmarked for India in the President's budget, and quiet negotiations for military sales appear to be in progress. Trade has improved modestly, but not impressively. Undoubtedly the crises in southern Africa, the Arab-Israeli dispute, oil and energy policies in general, Iran's forward policy from Turkey through Pakistan to India, the Eurocommunism issue, to say nothing of critical issues on the U.S. domestic front, demand high priority, and have left little time to nurture relations with India.

President Carter nevertheless did select India as one of the few stops on his winter 1977/1978 foreign tour, and Prime Minister Desai is expected to come to Washington in the summer of 1978. The President's state visit to New Delhi deserves analysis. He was well received by the public and by the government—more so, according to local reports, than was Britain's Prime Minister James Callaghan in his visit that followed shortly afterward.

Study is warranted of the two major documents that resulted from Carter's New Delhi discussions. The first was the President's speech before the Parliament of India on January 2, 1978. It is to be noted that the address was thoroughly cordial in tone and in its reception, and was even sentimental in places. Mr. Carter enunciated most of

XVIII · THE CARTER ADMINISTRATION AND INDIA

the clichés—India as the "largest democracy" in the world, the importance of democracy and economic development for all peoples, and the nature of the two countries' shared interests and obligations. Only a few paragraphs outlined more specific propositions.

One of these indirectly recognized the dominant role of India in South Asia, and gave some weight to the argument that India was a country of global importance. The key sentences were as follows:

> In global politics, history has cast our countries in different roles. The United States is one of the so-called superpowers; India is the largest of the nonaligned countries. But each of us respects the other's conception of its international responsibilities and the values that we do share provide a basis for cooperation in attacking the great global problems of economic justice, human rights, and the prevention of war.

Further on, President Carter said:

> Because India is both a developing country and also an industrial power, you are in a unique position to promote constructive international discussions about trade, energy, investment, balance of payments, technology, and other questions. I welcome your playing this worldwide leadership role.

This second statement gives every appearance of being an invitation to India to initiate negotiations for a "new economic order" in the world, with cooperation to be anticipated from the United States. Nothing was said, however, about India's peacekeeping role or its defense arrangements in the region.

Defense concerns, the prospects for economic aid, details on improved trade, and commitments of a firmer kind for improving Indo-American relations were noticeably

THE CARTER ADMINISTRATION AND INDIA · XIX

absent from the address, although these points may well have been raised in private discussions.

Mr. Carter's only direct reference to defense concerned nuclear weapons and peace:

> We are . . . working hard to restrict the proliferation of nuclear explosives. We are seeking to help the process of peace in Africa and the Middle East. And we are taking steps to forestall, along with the Soviets, great-power rivalry and the escalation of military presence in your own Indian Ocean.

Earlier in his address, the President noted that the United States would be shipping nuclear fuel and heavy water for certain of India's nuclear energy programs. (These remarks were essential to offset the President's private comment made to Secretary of State Vance—and heard by many over an open public address system—that a "blunt" letter must be sent to Prime Minister Desai on certain nuclear development matters in dispute between the two countries.)

The second document emerging from President Carter's visit was the "Delhi Declaration" of January 3, 1978, signed by Carter and Desai. It is a thoughtful and even elegant statement of the fundamentals of democracy, but it contains almost nothing of substance beyond good intentions. The basic principles of the United Nations relating to the peaceful settlement of disputes are highlighted, to which is added this key paragraph on disarmament:

> The spectre of war has hung over the world for too long. Existing stockpiles of nuclear weapons must be reduced and eventually eliminated, and the danger of proliferation of nuclear weapons must be arrested. Further, every effort must be made to progressively reduce conven-

tional arms and to redirect the productive forces so released to the betterment of mankind. We commit ourselves to work toward these ends.

The statement on the general reduction of nuclear as well as conventional weapons by *all* was introduced to make explicit one of India's chief criticisms of the Non-Proliferation Treaty, namely, that the superpowers and other major nuclear powers were doing too little in their own massive military systems to reduce the greatest threat to world security.

Ambassador Nani A. Palkhivala, in distributing copies of the "Delhi Declaration" to friends, had this to say about it:

The Delhi Declaration is unlike a normal joint communique. It does not refer to specific bilateral or current international situations. In the Declaration the world's two largest democracies have affirmed their deep commitment to fundamental freedoms for individuals, their respect for the worth and dignity of the human person, their faith in democracy, their emphasis on tolerance in a diverse and complex world, and their determination that all problems, wherever they exist, should be resolved through peaceful means alone.

IV

These surely are important general conclusions reached by leaders of two of the world's great powers. It remains, however, for them to grapple with nuclear energy, nuclear and conventional defense, aid, trade, and international political issues at greater depth, and in terms of mutually acceptable solutions. These themes may be expected to arise during future Indo-American negotiations, starting with Morarji Desai's planned visit to Washington in the summer of 1978.

The chapters that follow present details on India's strategic policies and plans that are reflected only dimly in the New Delhi documents of January 1978. U.S. strategic policies also were understated in New Delhi, as could be expected. Students of international security affairs, however, must probe beneath the surface of general public statements to find the roots of future differences and potential conflicts. That such differences exist will be made clear in this study. It is to be noted that President Carter and Prime Minister Desai recognized that the two countries would disagree on some issues, but the two leaders affirmed that the disagreements would arise in the context of a broader accord on the fundamentals of democratic societies.

CHAPTER 1
India's Status As A World Power

Studies of strategic power in world politics commonly assign to India the status of a middle power of some regional significance, but little more.[1] This paper is addressed to an examination of this issue. Two questions are central:
1. Is India an emergent power—in effect, a country of substantial strategic importance now, and of even greater potential importance?
2. If so, what are the policy implications for the United States?

The way that the questions are posed reflects the authors' belief that the answer to the first question is a qualified "yes," and thus that it is important for the United States to face more firmly the second question.

We are not unmindful of the ambiguities, qualifications, contrary evidence, and observers' biases that tend to surround these themes. Our conclusions may appear to be softened by exceptions and hypothetical propositions of

---

1. For example, Ray Cline barely ranks India ahead of Pakistan in terms of overall "perceived power," and behind it in military capability. This is not his most egregious error; such states as Quatar, Burma, and Yemen all rank ahead of Japan on the same scale! See Ray S. Cline, *World Power Assessment: A Calculus of Strategic Drift* (Boulder: Westview Press, 1975), pp. 85–86.

the "if, then that" variety. Such caution is necessary and appropriate in the Indian case, but analytical complications or a paucity of pointed evidence should not put off the careful strategic study of one of the world's major countries, even if the conclusions reached are tentative.

India's Shadow Image

Jawaharlal Nehru's encouragement of nonalignment during the bitter early years of the Cold War was construed as muddleheaded at best, or provocative and dangerous at worst, by both the Soviet Union and the United States. The fact that nonalignment and policies developed outside the direct influence of the superpowers have since been adopted by most of the countries of the developing world has not redounded to India's credit. On the contrary, the nonaligned now are seen as a power bloc of the relatively weak exercising pressures against the industrialized states through instrumentalities such as the "Group of 77" (now 115 countries) in the General Assembly of the United Nations.[2] Whereas the USSR and, to a lesser extent, the People's Republic of China, have since reacted positively, if selectively, to the policies of the nonaligned, the United States and most of its allies initially adjusted to nonalignment policies and their derivatives somewhat gracelessly, but with significant contributions in economic aid to key countries not opposed fundamentally to U.S. policies. India, as the largest of the

---

2. A detailed and affirmative assessment of the role of the nonaligned in world affairs is given in Jayantanuja Bandyopadhyay, "The Non-Aligned Movement and International Relations," *India Quarterly* (New Delhi) 33, no. 2 (April–June 1977), pp. 137–64.

nonaligned, has become a symbol of unwanted centers of assertive independence that permeate world affairs at a time when nuclear deterrence threatens global holocaust, and when the need for cooperation and economic interdependence would seem to demand that leadership by the advanced countries be accepted.

Skepticism concerning India's role in the world is enhanced by the economic crises that have become a way of life in the subcontinent, exacerbated by birth-death rates that will lift India's population to one billion by the end of the century. In addition to the economic factors that are thought to reduce the country's effectiveness in maintaining logistical support for a modern defense force, critics note that India: did not sign the Non-Proliferation Treaty (NPT); became a nuclear power after the testing of an atomic device in the Rajasthan desert in 1974; has fought four wars with immediate neighbors in thirty years (Pakistan in 1947–48, 1965, 1971; China in 1962); and tainted its standing among the nonaligned by signing the Treaty of Peace, Friendship and Cooperation with the USSR in 1971. Moreover, in the exercise of military power, detractors note the undistinguished quality of India's battles against Pakistan in 1947–48 and 1965, balanced in part by the Bangladesh liberation war of 1971—carried out with precision but by a large Indian force against a much smaller, isolated Pakistani Army in East Bengal. As for the Sino-Indian border war of 1962, it was a debacle for India from any point of view.

Western perceptions of India take into account the factors outlined above; add the long-standing left-socialist inclinations of some of India's leaders; recall the political, social, and economic instabilities of the country (exemplified by the Emergency of Indira Gandhi, 1975–1977);

and conclude that India is, par excellence, a country that should devote concentrated attention to its internal problems of political stability, social change, regional integration, and economic growth. India, in this perspective, has only a modest role to play in the realm of world affairs.

India's Worldview

Indian spokesmen deny few of the critical points so far raised, although interpretations differ radically on specific cases. Certainly foreign affairs is seen in a totally different light and is given a much higher level of priority.

Gandhi and some of his successors favored an India that was inward-looking, decentralized in its distribution of power, and relatively untied to the world of power politics. But Gandhi also deferred to Jawaharlal Nehru in the construction of the bases of India's defense, foreign, and international economic policies. Nehru set the framework for an active external policy that those who followed him as prime minister—Lal Bahadur Shastri (1964–66), Indira Gandhi (1966–77), and Morarji Desai (1977–)—have continued, with only minor changes. Nehru's worldview linked closely the internal interests of India with external policies.[3]

It was essential, in India's view of the world, for national security to be sought by a defense force adequate to

---

3. The best source remains Nehru's own writings, especially the concluding chapters of *Toward Freedom: The Autobiography of Jawaharlal Nehru* (New York: John Day, 1941), and *The Discovery of India* (New York: John Day, 1946), both of which are available in several editions. See also Nehru's *India's Foreign Policy: Selected Speeches, September 1946–April 1961* (New Delhi: Government of India, Publications Division, Ministry of Information and Broadcasting, 1961).

protect India's interests at home. This need was made abundantly clear by the nation's military weakness shown in its wars with Pakistan and, most sharply, by its border war with China in 1962. Internal defense then must be tied to the shaping of arrangements in international affairs, especially in Asia and the Pacific, that would reduce conditions likely to lead to serious outbreaks of violence, thus potentially threatening India. One critical early step was to consolidate its territory (Kashmir, Hyderabad, Junagadh, French and Portuguese India, Sikkim) and protect its borders (with Pakistan, East Bengal, Burma, China, Nepal, and Bhutan). At the same time, active involvement in the United Nations on a worldwide scale, regional concern with Asia and the Middle East, and leadership among the developing countries provided means for altering international economic structures that tended to favor the strong over the weak. Finally, India spread a wide diplomatic network around the world and engaged in bilateral relations—political, cultural, and economic—with a great number of countries, large and small, on all continents.

The fact is that there has been a consistency in India's policies of national centralization and unification since independence, as well as a foreign policy that has been global in its objectives.[4] Criticism from outsiders has not deflected India from its recognition of itself as a major nation that has achieved great power status.[5]

---

4. The global objectives of India's foreign policy are reviewed in the context of Asian relations by Richard L. Park, "India's Asian Relations," in George T. Yu, ed., *Intra-Asian International Relations* (Boulder: Westview Press, 1977).

5. A more tentative conclusion concerning India's current status as a great power will be found in D. K. Palit (retired Major-General), "India as an Asian Military Power," *India International Centre Quarterly* 2, no. 1 (January 1975), pp. 35–47.

India as a Great Power

Great power status can imply regional, continental, or global influence. At minimum it means regional hegemony, which India in large part has acquired. The next stage—dominance in Asia—clearly is beyond its grasp. Extra-regional influence, however, is possible for India, and indeed now is exercised with moderate success. India's regional hegemony has been slow in coming, for it was dependent upon the acquisition of a number of capabilities. India has had to master the twin domestic crises of economic development and national integration, and it must resist outside penetration of its own political system and deter outside powers from lending support to regional competitors. It has also had to develop an awareness that these capabilities exist and acquire the will to exercise power in such a way as to achieve or maintain hegemony over regional competitors.

Regional hegemony or dominance thus implies the existence of local military preponderance over neighbors through the spectrum of force, the availability of nonmilitary instruments of pressure (including inducement and economic coercion), the ability to influence the consequences following upon domestic political weaknesses in rival regional states, and a willingness to conduct a strategy of diplomacy that places regional dominance above other objectives. A state such as India, by virtue of its size, resources, and geographic location, finds itself a great power in regional terms, whether or not it seeks the label, and despite the fact that all of its capabilities for regional dominance are not yet fully secured. India's current preeminence over its neighbors, however, is so substantial that its position has been recognized by all major outside powers, and implicitly so by all South Asian states as well, even including Pakistan.

The acquisition of extra-regional—continental or global—influence will require other capacities. For India, it demands a firm regional base in South Asia, since local hegemony is a prerequisite for broader ambitions. Nehru's attempt to build a recognized global role for India failed less because of the imaginativeness of his vision than because of the widespread recognition after 1962 that India was not master in its own house. An extra-regional position nevertheless does require such a vision of a broader role: of a destiny waiting to be fulfilled.

Such a claim to great power status may not be based entirely upon military prowess (although that inevitably is a component of the claim), but also upon a distinctive ideological or political role which finds harmonic resonance in states outside the region. Military power can be enlisted in the service of such a vision in a number of ways: clients and allies can receive arms assistance or be permitted to purchase weaponry; training programs can establish direct links between friendly military establishments; officers and crews can be loaned, even for long periods of time, for training or actual combat purposes; naval visits can be arranged for symbolic purposes; and there may be some scope for more direct, overt military involvement. India has used its military power in most of these ways, but less in the service of extra-regional ambitions than as a way of weakening outside support for Pakistan. Similarly, opening access to economic resources and technological skills, the shaping of patterns of trade, the granting of credit, and the sale of goods at favorable rates supplement military power in undergirding great power status within and beyond the regional base. India has utilized economic means for enhancing its power for many years—limited, of course, by the enormous internal demands for scarce resources.

CHAPTER 2

Analytical Perspectives

Resources and Leadership

Geostrategic Location

It is not unusual for Indian and foreign analysts to overstress the importance of the subcontinent's geographic and strategic position between Europe (plus the Middle East) and Asia, including its close proximity to both the USSR and China. Evaluations of such locational factors were more applicable to India in the nineteenth century: before the coming of the jet-ICBM-nuclear age; before the decline of mountains and oceans as natural protective devices; and before the reduction in the role of seapower as a critical military and commercial force. If the nuclear genie is released from the bottle, there is, indeed, no place to hide. Moreover, even in situations of conventional conflict, the speed and capabilities of modern air and missile power outdate earlier conceptions of India's relative security; conversely, the same conclusions provide India with potential roles in world affairs far distant from its own shores. One has no reason to give undue weight to India's strategic location.

It is true, nevertheless, that India's borders do abut for

long distances those of the People's Republic of China (P.R.C.), and that the USSR is a close neighbor. Tests with China over borderlands have been several since 1947, especially relating to Tibet in the early 1950s, and over the Aksai Chin area of Ladakh and the Northeast Frontier in the early 1960s. Even now, both the P.R.C. and India maintain military border guards of substantial size.

In a broader sense, India has become a marginally significant segment of the Sino-Soviet dispute. At the moment, India's stronger supportive relationship rests with the USSR, but the exchange of ambassadors between India and the P.R.C. in 1976 may introduce a fresh phase of Indo-Soviet and Sino-Indian relations that could lead to the neutralization of South Asia as a potential factor in Sino-Soviet conflicts.

The most crucial geopolitical factor of the subcontinent, however, is the central, dominating position of India. This region of some 800 million people constitutes a sizable portion of the world's population. It makes a difference whether or not the peoples of South Asia work out their problems and differences amicably and effectively. India, more than any other power, will determine these outcomes.

Economic Base

The economy of India has made great strides since 1947 in agricultural growth, in industrialization, and in the development of modern transportation facilities, energy, and trained manpower, to cite a few of its achievements.[6] The

---

[6]. For examinations of India's economic development since 1947, see Jagdish N. Bhagwati and Padma Desai, *India: Planning for Industrialization: Industrialization and Trade Policies since 1951* (New York: Oxford University Press, 1970); Francine R. Frankel, *India's Green Revolution: Economic Gains and Political Costs*

fact remains, however, that the country is poor, despite the existence of highly developed sectors in the economy: per capita annual income does not exceed $150; investment levels are limited; production rates in the factories and on the land are not up to planned expectations; deficit budgets have been regular; payments of interest and principal on external debts are rising; educational institutions have not retooled adequately to produce the specialized personnel needed for more rapid growth. These are fundamental economic problems that will require decades to solve.

At the same time, even if the overall economic base is not strong enough for the people being served, thirty years of development since independence have given to India segments of industrial production that are the rough equivalent in quality and sophistication to any in the world, as well as increasing agricultural yields when the monsoons have been good. Even the export-import balance has been more acceptable in recent years, as have been balances in foreign exchange. In rough and ready terms, India's performance compares with that of China—more perhaps in agriculture than in industry—but much remains to be done to improve the lot of the vast bulk of the people who remain poor. It is in the distribution of the results of economic growth where China and India differ most, and the evidence favors China in this comparison.

It is important to note that the basic economic weaknesses of India have not prevented the building of a large,

---

(Princeton: Princeton University Press, 1971); George Rosen, *Democracy and Economic Change in India,* rev. ed. (Berkeley: University of California Press, 1967); and Lawrence A. Veit, *India's Second Revolution: The Dimensions of Development* (New York: McGraw-Hill, 1976).

modernized defense force, supported by an iron and steel industry, related industrial support plants, a munitions industry, centers for the training of scientific and technological personnel, and the reasonably rapid expansion of a middle class management group quite capable of handling the complexities of leadership for an aspiring great power. In economic power India is at least the equivalent of a middle-sized European country, despite the gross problems of the development which is needed to provide appropriate support to the 80 percent of the population who are poor. Furthermore, as later discussion will point out, economic resources used in support of military objectives may speed up rather than impede civilian economic growth. Poverty, as a statistical fact, based on the mean, need not obviate great power status. India is a classic example of this phenomenon.

Political System

India has managed to operate a complex, constitutional, federal, parliamentary, party-dominated political system with remarkable effectiveness since 1947, even taking into account the attempt during the 1975–1977 Emergency to impose more authoritarian styles of rule.[7] Future political crises no doubt loom, but this can only be expected considering the country's social and economic stresses. There is no reason to believe, at least at this stage, that the Indian democratic system of government will collapse.

The country is favored by hundreds of thousands of able politicians, civil servants, engineers, scientists, and mana-

---

7. For one example of the literature on the Emergency period, see Henry C. Hart, ed., *Indira Gandhi's India: A Political System Reappraised* (Boulder: Westview Press, 1976).

gers. India's civilian political leaders in New Delhi have held a firm hand on the making of both foreign and defense policies, and have not allowed the military to overstep their roles as advisers on policy, and as commanders only in times of conflict—and even then the military has operated under political direction. The making of foreign and defense policies has been recognized by India's political leaders as critical in the management of domestic affairs as well. A neo-Gandhian prime minister, such as Morarji Desai, might prefer not to be responsible for the making of military decisions, but his administrative and political experience reveals a man prepared to use a tough hand in this area, if the necessity arises.[8]

It is unlikely that military rule will come to the fore in India—a remarkable exception in the developing world where military domination (or military power exercised politically behind the scenes) has been more usual than exceptional. At the same time, arms levels (including nuclear capabilities) are likely to remain substantial for many years to come, supported by a linkage of interests between key civil servants, military leaders, industrial managers, and top-level politicians.

Military Capabilities

Analytic and Perceptual Obstacles

While it is difficult even for a professional soldier to evaluate accurately the military capabilities of any country, there are special obstacles in the case of India. These per-

---

8. See Morarji Desai, *The Story of My Life*, 2 vols. (Madras: Macmillan India, 1974).

tain to the quantity and quality of information available, perceptual screens erected by Indians and non-Indians, and the standards of judgment that appropriately may be applied to the Indian case.

Although India has been a relatively open democracy (except for the Emergency period of 1975–77), there is no question that its political leaders have maintained a highly restrictive information policy concerning defense and security. Successive Indian governments have been obsessed with the issue of military secrecy, shielding the Indian officer corps from outside view, restricting access of foreigner and Indian alike.[9] Only since the 1960s have security studies been taken seriously in India. In some areas—e.g., recruitment or the structure of the military—there was greater parliamentary and press interest under British rule than there is now. While the Indian government may have cause to be concerned about outside access to the armed forces (they were aware of the ties of the military to outsiders in neighboring Pakistan during the 1950s), they are equally fearful that defense matters will become a domestic political issue, and thus have sought to dampen potential criticism by a controlled flow of information.

There are other obstacles to an appreciation of India's true military strength. India has long been linked to "Gandhism," pacifism, and nonviolence in the minds of many foreign observers; and its governments have been

---

9. One notable exception was Neville Maxwell, *The Times* (London) correspondent in New Delhi, who apparently used highly classified materials in *India's China War* (London: Jonathan Cape, 1970), a book highly critical of Indian policy.

reluctant to tamper with the view that India's security and military policies somehow were more enlightened or more moral than those of other states. This in turn has led to excessive disappointment and criticism of India by liberals and conservatives alike following the 1962 defeat by China. The liberals have come to see India as the aggressor in that conflict; the conservatives see India as a weak and incompetent victim. As a result, it has become more difficult for many to comprehend Indian strategic planning when India rearmed and accepted assistance from both East and West, still under the guise of nonalignment. India's international image became blurred and contradictory, seemingly composed of incompatible traits and characteristics: the land of Gandhi embarking upon a military expansion program in the name of an increasingly flexible policy of nonalignment.

A final hindrance to our understanding of India's military strength lies in questions surrounding the choice of standards to be applied. For most nations, the military need only be powerful enough to maintain law and order and to deter limited incursions. India, however, stands midway between the pygmies and the giants: it interacts closely with neighboring micro-states and weak nations on the one hand (Nepal, Bhutan, Sri Lanka), and the superpowers on the other. Additionally, it has faced periodic military confrontations with a middle-sized state, Pakistan, and with its own Asian giant twin, China. Therefore, in the following discussion, it should be borne in mind that India's military power, even at its weakest, may be more than adequate for certain regional relationships, and its potential power, even at its greatest, may be inadequate for confrontations with a superpower.

Resources Applied to Security

Estimates of Indian military power tend to one of two common errors. The first, usually committed by foreign observers, is to underestimate the social, economic, and technological resources available for security purposes, while overestimating India's poverty, lack of discipline, and disunity. The second, usually committed by otherwise well-informed Indians, is to exaggerate the importance of sheer size and India's "special" territorial position, while underestimating—perhaps wishfully—the difficulty of translating existing material strength into military power.

A more accurate characterization of Indian capabilities and resources is that of Emile Benoit:

> In consequence of its vast population and substantial GNP, India, like Mainland China, is able to maintain a modern advanced sector in the midst of its prevailing poverty, and this sector is, in absolute size, larger than that of many far more advanced but smaller countries.[10]

Like China, the special advantage of India lies in a successful combination of the material resources, technology, and organizational skills of the "modern advanced sector," with enormous manpower resources available at relatively low cost. This has permitted the maintenance of *both* sophisticated arms (armor, aircraft, naval forces) and a sizable standing army. It also means that, on a gross level of cost analysis, India's defense burden is relatively modest.

As the tables in Appendix A (pp. 77–79) indicate, India stands somewhere near the center of the countries listed in

---

10. *Defense and Economic Growth in Developing Countries* (Lexington: Lexington Books, 1973).

terms of its military expenditures as a percentage of GNP. For the past ten years this has ranged between 3.5 percent and 3.9 percent. Considering only the states with substantial military establishments (above 100,000 soldiers), India's expenditure per soldier ranks in the low-to-middle category. On a $ *per head* basis, expenditures are among the lowest in the world ($4 per person). The fact that India's 630 million people (as of 1977) earn only about $150 per person per annum reduces the drama of the $4 per head figure, however.

These comparative data do not indicate certain additional defense costs, such as the drain on foreign exchange. Japan, for example, expends considerable amounts of foreign currency on security, but can easily afford to do so. India, by contrast, faces a much tighter foreign exchange situation, and must continually balance developmental and defense demands for such funds.

One would expect that the developmental and defense objectives necessarily would be in conflict, but Benoit's study of the problem indicates that the contrary may be true. In the 1960s, India was a "loose" state in which greater defense efforts might have had a *positive* relationship to economic growth, unlike more developed systems in which defense expenditures compete directly with developmental efforts. The added rigor, discipline, compulsion, and patriotic incentives that were associated with the increased Indian defense effort after 1962 may themselves have contributed to overall economic growth, more than compensating for the diversion of foreign exchange.[11]

---

11. This point has been made by several Indian writers who have argued against cuts in the defense budget. Lawrence A. Veit, in his recent study of the Indian economy, takes exception to Benoit's conclusions, and states his belief that, even at low rates of return, India's growth would have been greater had

18 · INDIA: EMERGENT POWER?

The Indian defense build-up (which began even before 1962) was indeed comprehensive. Under V.K. Krishna Menon's guidance, the defense production base was expanded rapidly, and a vast system of defense industries was installed by the late 1960s. These industries were largely the consequence of Jawaharlal Nehru's particular view of the defense requirements of India. Nehru long had advocated the industrial route to both national economic development and defense. Aware of the requirements of modern warfare, he favored the establishment of an Indian industrial base upon which could be built an autonomous defense superstructure. The war with China in 1962 disrupted his timetable, and India was forced to obtain whole weapons systems, as well as quantities of light arms, ammunition, and other military supplies, from foreign sources. Thus, approximately ten complete Indian mountain divisions were equipped with American supplies, and the Indian Air Force received Soviet helicopters and MiG 21 interceptors. The Indian Navy earlier (1960–61) had purchased several British ships. Nonetheless, given a choice, India has preferred to acquire manufacturing facilities—by grant or either rupee or hard currency purchase. Most of the major weapons programs undertaken by India have been characterized by a gradual accumulation of Indian expertise: a tank factory developed in cooperation with Vickers of Great Britain; three linked MiG factories built by the Soviet Union; and the Leander class frigate program, started with British assistance. As Appendix B (pp. 80–83) indicates, there are other programs, and virtually all of them provide for an increasing Indian

---

defense funds been diverted to the civilian economy. See *India's Second Revolution: The Dimensions of Development* (New York: McGraw-Hill, 1976), pp. 110–115.

contribution in the design, engineering, and manufacture of a particular weapon. At the present time, India produces, in whole or in part, several types of combat aircraft, the Vickers tank, light training aircraft, a complete range of small arms, artillery, and ammunition, and a variety of small and medium-sized naval vessels. (Sounding rockets and missiles also appear to be forthcoming.) Indian officials often claim that one or another weapon is 90 percent or 95 percent indigenous, although it usually is not clear whether or not the imported 5 or 10 percent constitutes some vital or essential component of the complete system, thus making India vulnerable—by virtue of its need for spare parts and components—to foreign control.

In sum, India is one of the very few of the "poorer" nations of the world with a substantial indigenous military manufacturing capability. It is fully comparable to China in this regard. This has several important political and strategic consequences.

Firstly, India is on the verge of entering the arms export market in a substantial way. There already has been at least one major sale to the Persian Gulf (50 tanks to Kuwait), and attempts to sell MiGs or spare parts to Egypt.[12] Other efforts may also have taken place. India may be able to compete favorably in some ways in the world's arms market. Secondly, India's defense industry is based on a substantial industrial capacity and further

---

12. India hopes to balance out defense imports (approximately $200 million per year) with an arms export program. One selling point presumably would be that as an experienced victim of "strings" attached to weapons received from abroad, India in contrast would be liberal in its customers' use of Indian-supplied equipment. The Soviet Union has blocked Indian attempts to sell spare parts for MiGs that have been manufactured under license. *Far Eastern Economic Review* (Hong Kong), June 3, 1977, and July 8, 1977.

growth can be expected. India is a long way from autonomy, but is beginning to design and construct a number of military items from scratch. Particular weaknesses are in the areas of electronics, communications equipment, metal fabrication, and high quality steels. Thirdly, the defense industry is largely state-owned or, when part of the private sector, state-dominated. This has given rise to a massive bureaucratic-military-industrial complex that differs strikingly from its American counterpart in its autonomy from the electoral political system. It is a vast, powerful industrial empire, with direct ties to the central government and the military, and can be expected to influence future strategic decisions by its promise of increasing capability.

India's Armed Forces

While they are not particularly powerful when compared with the United States or the USSR, India's armed forces are large and more than adequate to meet most threats to Indian security. Conventionally organized into three separate armed services, the manpower strength of the military has remained fairly constant for ten years at 1,000,000, although a process of upgrading equipment has necessitated continual qualitative improvement.

Historically, the army has held pride of place in South Asia. Developed by the British as an internal security and expeditionary force, the Indian Army traces its origins to the eighteenth century, and, in terms of manpower, is now the world's third largest land army. It is organized into two armored divisions, approximately sixteen infantry divisions, with thirteen independent infantry and armor brigades, and an additional ten mountain divisions. The latter are simply conventional infantry divisions stripped of most of their transport and heavy equipment, and deployed in the Himalayas against considerably smaller Pakistani and Chinese frontier forces.

The army retains much of its caste-based organizational structure, which has not detracted from its fighting capacity. This system, unique to South Asia, is characterized by the use of a combination of *jawans* (the Indian GI) drawn primarily from the village peasantry, with officers recruited from the middle and upper classes of Indian society. The army is held together by these officers, who are recruited and trained by means of the English language. Without their careful leadership, the army itself would be prone to disintegration along regional and caste lines. For both army officer and *jawan,* and for the other two services, the military is seen as a career, and there is no conscription. While attempts have been made to broaden its base, the army still is drawn largely from the regions of India which traditionally supplied recruits for the British; the officer corps is more representative, however, and is one of the genuinely all-Indian institutions in recruitment and outlook.

India's second most powerful service, the air force, is (like the navy) patterned after Western models. There is no specific caste recruitment to these two services, and educational requirements are substantially higher than for the army. Enlisted personnel and officers tend to come from the great urban centers (Bombay, Calcutta, Madras). As indicated in Appendix C (pp. 84–86), India's air power is unbalanced. Light interceptors predominate, and there is a noticeable shortage of all-weather sophisticated attack aircraft. To some extent this deficiency is made up by updated versions of the Gnat ("Ajeet") and MiG 21, which permit a ground support role.[13] There are also very few medium bombers, as well as deficiencies in air reconnaissance and in helicopter strength.

The weakest service has been the navy, which is also the youngest. Many of its major ships are aging World War II combatants; a few antedate 1939. For years the navy was deliberately starved of funds for the simple reason that strategic threats were thought to be exclusively across land frontiers. The 1971 Bangladesh struggle—and the intervention of the U.S. *Enterprise* and its supporting vessels—transformed Indian thinking on the subject, and the work of one of India's strongest advocates of seapower, K.M. Panikkar, was reevaluated. Capital costs remain high, however, and the debate within the Indian Navy over its priorities did not reach any strong consensus between those who wished to acquire a "two ocean" fleet, implying the acquisition of a second aircraft carrier, and those who saw the future in small surface and coastal vessels, a frigate fleet, and submarines—i.e., essentially a defensive navy. The compromise that seems to have been reached is the retention of the single carrier, INS *Vikrant*, and the acquisition of an Indian submarine building capacity to complement the frigate program.

As we have noted, the officer corps for each of the three services is centrally recruited and trained by the English language medium. Their rank structure is derived from Western models, as is the extensive system of service academies, schools, and other training institutions. Most of these have been functioning under complete Indian

---

13. According to numerous press reports, India has been searching for a modern attack fighter for many years. However, since it is interested in joint or local production, this has proven to be difficult to achieve. A comprehensive analysis is in *Air International*, October 1975, pp. 170–79.

control since independence. There is no question about the competence of Indian military leadership, or the capacity of the military to restructure itself after a calamity such as the 1962 war with China. Indian generalship may not be inspired, but it is better than adequate. The officer corps of the army, navy, and air force thus constitute an area of high level organizational expertise in a country not especially noted for these skills. The officers are fully professionalized, along Western lines, and—perhaps unique among developing states—remain carefully subordinate to civilian direction and control.

While formal civilian control is exercised through a series of legal, constitutional, and organizational arrangements, the informal control mechanisms are equally important. Promotions at the higher ranks are made by civilians; training and indoctrination of officers are civilian-guided; informal rewards and punishments are available to bring recalcitrant officers, including generals, into line; and—above all—civilian competence in a number of areas vital to national security remains of a high quality. These competencies include foreign policy expertise, management of the defense budget, control over the defense manufacturing and scientific research empire, and management of the political system itself. What incentive is there for a well paid, well trained, and reasonably well equipped soldier to challenge civilian authority? In recent years, very little. The examples of the difficulties faced by soldier-politicians in neighboring Pakistan, Bangladesh, and Burma serve as stern deterrents to a military coup. Barring some major domestic calamity or massive military defeat, civilian control is likely to remain an important feature of India's security system. This means that the use of the military abroad, the structure of the defense establishment, the acquisition and development of weaponry, including nuclear forces, and the symbolic and actual use of the military *within* India will be determined primarily by civilians applying civilian criteria. The armed forces constitute an interest group within Indian society, and an important and growing component of that society. They do not determine, however, vital matters of security and strategy; they are subject to civilian control and direction in a way fully comparable to the Western democracies.

Our analysis of India's military capability leads us to the preliminary conclusion that it remains a potential rather than actual great power in military terms. With such a large population and industrial base, the possibility will always remain that additional massive indigenous resources could be allocated to the military. However, India's present political system is not likely to be able to extract such resources without a radical change in state and party structure. Even during the recent flirtation with authoritarianism, it became apparent that New Delhi's political leadership was unable or unwilling to disrupt India's middle class or its wealthier peasantry by higher taxation, despite the fact that these groups had otherwise profited from or supported the Emergency. Agricultural and rural wealth generally is notably undertaxed in India, but it would take years before the coercive machinery could be created that would yield substantially greater revenues from the countryside. The reason that the above conclusion must remain preliminary is that India's military power cannot be fully appreciated without an evaluation of the power of neighboring and competing states. We now turn to such an evaluation, with special focus on India's relations with its historical antagonist, Pakistan, and its Asian twin giant, China.

India and Its Neighbors: Conflict, Competition, and Cooperation

Our observations about India's military capabilities now can be placed within the context of the South Asian strategic environment. This environment is remarkably conflict-laden, and has been characterized by wars between India and its neighbors, the military involvement of the superpowers in the region, and numerous smaller scaled military actions. Yet, despite this history of war and conflict, the regional states do engage each other in peaceful competition, as well as in a remarkably large amount of outright cooperation.

The following analysis necessarily is brief. We will argue that India's regional relationships are extraordinarily complex, and by extension amenable to discussion, negotiation, and peaceful change, as well as to the application or threat of violence. We will also use the conflicts of the past as benchmarks by which India's expanding strategic capabilities can be measured; the critical question being whether or not India can hope to dominate its own region, the minimum condition for great power status.

India and Pakistan: The Basic Axis

There are those in both India and Pakistan who envision a future subcontinental holocaust. They liken the future relationship between the two states to a massive communal riot between Hindus and Muslims, tanks and aircraft substituting for clubs and stones. This apocalyptic vision is neither realistic nor accurate. There are cultural attractions as well as repulsions between India and Pakistan, and both have their origins deep in subcontinental history. There are, for example, shared treasures in the spheres of music, literature, language, and cuisine, as well as more unpleasant memories. Before the British established their authority, much of India was dominated by a series of continental and regional Islamic imperial systems; this rule was accompanied by conversion from Hinduism to Islam, especially in Bengal and Punjab. This legacy of Islamic attraction and former dominance is recalled with mixed emotion by Hindu and Muslim alike, and occasionally bubbles to the surface in the outpourings of extremist groups on both sides.

The fact that India and Pakistan are relatively new states, still groping for a viable identity, has also plagued their relationships, and there are those on each side who deny the legitimacy of the other. Pakistan was formed as a home for the Muslims of South Asia, yet many live protected and content in secular India. Conversely, a large number of Hindus remained after partition in East Bengal (now Bangladesh). In a sense, the minority communities in Pakistan and India were hostages for each other.

Such aspects of Indian and Pakistani identity have had a strong impact on their foreign policies. To reassure their Muslim minority that opposition to Pakistan was not based on hatred of Muslims, India has gone out of its way to maintain cordial ties with the Arab states. Many Indian leaders regard Israel as a Middle Eastern analogue to Pakistan: a state artificially created to serve the ends of a particular religious group. (Some Hindu groups, impatient with Indian secularism, are attracted to Israel for this very reason.) Pakistan's desire to develop support among other Muslim states has led it to a strong pro-Arab policy, and for many years both India and Pakistan have competed for Arab favor, and more recently for the favor of

Iran. Such competition now has an economic twist, since both states remain dependent upon Middle Eastern oil.

The hostility of India and Pakistan has had important economic consequences. Partition in 1947 cut across economic arteries: it led to the destruction of an integrated jute industry and river transport system in East and West Bengal, and of the railway, road, and canal systems of Punjab. It also meant the loss of skilled managerial personnel for Pakistan (again, primarily in the East). Even today, the scars of partition remain: Pakistan's international air traffic can be disrupted readily by India; and a dispute remains over the flow of water from India through Bangladesh, and India's diversion of that water by means of the Farakka Barrage. (The Farakka dispute has moved closer to settlement by the signing of an agreement by India and Bangladesh on November 5, 1977.) Economic cooperation between India and Pakistan also is minimal, although there is scope for the development of regional markets and tourism. The creation of such a system of cooperation inevitably will be determined by progress at political levels.

We have emphasized these cultural, economic, and psychological ties between India and Pakistan because they are of critical importance in the overall relationships of the countries. However, the two states have engaged each other as strategic opponents virtually since their creation in 1947, and relations between India and Pakistan now are highly militarized.

The partition of India in 1947 was carried out largely along communal and religious lines, with little or no regard for the future defenses of each state. It was assumed by the British that the security of the subcontinent would be jointly managed, and an attempt was made to bring the Pakistani and Indian armies under unified (British) direction. These efforts failed, and the two states early found themselves highly vulnerable to military threats, each from the other.

Pakistan was especially vulnerable, since several of its major cities (notably Lahore), irrigation canals, and key rail and road links are within easy reach of the Indian border. This unpleasant fact, coupled with an exaggerated notion of Muslim martial qualities, and possibly an adaptation of foreign military doctrine to the subcontinent, had early led Pakistan to a strategy of defending its own territory by attacking on Indian soil.[14] Modern armored forces require a substantial amount of space for maneuver, and such space simply was not available to Pakistan. On their side, the Indians were content for many years to accommodate such a strategy by trading space for time, and holding the main Indian armored units back in their central Indian cantonments. Thus, in 1964 (the Rann of Kutch), 1965, and 1971, it was the Pakistani forces that first struck in combined armor-air assaults, designed to slow down or deter any Indian plunge into Pakistan, as well as to bring the Indo-Pakistani struggle before an international forum. To this day, Pakistan regards a "deterrent" capability as vital for its own defense: such a deterrent would involve massive and deep penetration into Indian territory by armored and air units, destroying key transportation and military facilities, making it difficult for the Indian military machine to mount a successful counterattack, while diplomatic activity was directed toward obtaining a quick ceasefire. The Indian-controlled portions of

---

14. See Aslam Siddiqi, *Pakistan Seeks Security* (Lahore: Longmans Green, 1960).

Kashmir, now integrated into the Indian Union, are militarily vulnerable both to direct attack and to the severance of the tenuous road link from the plains. India has been constrained in its plans for counterattack by the need to maintain large bodies of troops to defend Kashmir and its access routes.

In a sense, such an arrangement has not been unacceptable, for it meant that no major population centers were attacked, and there was some measure of a tacit arms control agreement between the two states. Now, however, there may be some fundamental changes in this rough military standoff. India's superiority in airpower—now at least a 4:1 dominance, and constituting, on the whole, a more modern force, backed up by one of the world's most advanced air defense systems—means that any future armored thrust by Pakistan will be undertaken without meaningful air support. Further, since India is reported to have moved many of its armored units much closer to the Punjab-Rajasthan frontier, Indian reaction time would be very short in a future conflict. The resemblance to the Middle East military balance is striking, with both a decrease in warning time, and (because of the greater mobility and firepower of modern weapons) an increased risk of unacceptable damage should the enemy strike first.[15]

The shifting military balance between them has played an important role in the foreign policies of India and Pakistan. Because each might resort to force, negotiations always are carried out with one eye on this balance; and

---

15. For a discussion of the problem in abstract terms, see Robert Jervis, "Cooperation Under the Security Dilemma," Center for Arms Control and International Security, UCLA, Working Paper No. 4, April 1977.

relations with potential arms suppliers are matters of the first priority. Relations with the opponents' arms suppliers are no less critical, and much of the diplomacy of India and Pakistan continues to revolve around calculations of obtaining adequate outside support and military supplies, and denying them to the antagonist.

At various times each of the superpowers has become deeply involved in efforts to resolve the India-Pakistan dispute.[16] For a number of years the United States tried to play the sometimes conflicting roles of balancer, supplier, and mediator. These efforts faded after the 1965 war, as the relevance of the region to U.S. interests was thought to have declined and involvement in Vietnam grew. At that point, the Soviet Union took up the initiative, holding out offers of supplies and weapons to both states, if they agreed to forge a common front against China. Pakistan refused, as it refused to yield its position on Kashmir, and China became its leading weapons supplier for a number of years.[17] In all of this activity, the superpowers were concerned primarily with using India and Pakistan as counters to the other superpower, or to China. The basic India-Pakistan conflict made it impossible to realize the earlier British dream of a united subcontinent, but it also made it easier to acquire at least temporary influence through arms sales or grants, resulting in a highly militarized approach to foreign policy by all parties concerned.

---

16. For comprehensive studies, see William J. Barnds, *India, Pakistan and the Great Powers* (New York: Praeger, 1972), and G. W. Choudhury, *India, Pakistan, Bangladesh, and the Major Powers* (New York: Free Press, 1975).

17. Shivaji Ganguly, *Pakistan-China Relations: A Study in Interaction* (Urbana: University of Illinois, Center for Asian Studies, 1971), p. 22 ff.

As long as the basic conflict remains, it will be relatively easy for outside powers to involve themselves in regional politics, although the rewards are sufficiently limited that such involvement is likely to remain constrained.

A difference in the degree of dependence on external military support is a major factor in the India-Pakistan equation. India has the capacity to replenish much of its own arms inventories even with diminishing external assistance, and still has the better source of external weapons—the USSR. There are limits to Chinese capabilities as a supplier of weapons to Pakistan, and the equipment that has been provided is not very advanced or reliable. Pakistan has not acquired American weapons in substantial quantities since the late 1950s, and under present policy it will have to pay in hard currency for any fresh purchases. Indeed, American arms manufacturers have seen India as the better prospect in the region, and put pressure on the U.S. government in 1972 to lift an arms embargo as much to gain access to India as to Pakistan.[18]

Finally, one must take into consideration the likelihood of India becoming an expansionist power, particularly with regard to Pakistan. Until 1971 the question was dismissed with a brief comparison of military resources: India's superiority was only marginal. Additionally, Pakistan

---

18. In 1977 McDonnell-Douglas obtained permission to show the Indian government its A-4 (naval attack) aircraft. Presumably India would be interested in replacing its dwindling stock of Seahawks (an obsolete British plane that no longer is manufactured) with A-4s, and acquiring the A-4 production line. However, the latter plane may not be suitable for the *Vikrant*, and is itself approaching obsolescence. More recent reports indicate an interest in acquiring the British VTOL "jump-jet," the Harrier, a very expensive aircraft of limited performance capabilities.

could still claim the support (albeit unsteady) of both the U.S. and China, although neither offered substantial assistance in Pakistan's hour of greatest need. This latter development, plus India's increasing military superiority over Pakistan, permits us to think about the once unthinkable: what are the conditions under which India would be led again to war with Pakistan?

The motives for such an effort would seem to be twofold. Firstly, there might be a rerun of the Bangladesh episode in Pakistan. One or more regions of Pakistan might attempt to break away (presumably, Baluchistan or Sindh from Punjabi domination), and the possibility of civil war, massive internal disruption, and the destruction of the Pakistani political order might make Indian intervention, on balance, the lesser of two evils. However, the threshold of intervention would be much higher in this case than it was in 1971. There are no substantial Hindu minority groups in (West) Pakistan which might flee across the border, nor is disruption on one side of the border likely to inflame passion on the other. Finally, the regions of greatest trouble for Pakistan's central leadership are, with the exception of Azad Kashmir, not adjacent to India. Thus, on balance, a renewal of "1971-like" political struggle is not likely to involve an Indian intervention, especially if the Pakistani military continues to regard itself as the proper corrective agent.[19]

---

19. We take the present (military) leadership of Pakistan at its word, and assume that civilian government will indeed be established in the near future. However, the military will remain attentive to political and social disruption in Pakistan, and are likely to intervene again, if the politicians cannot manage the country. For a thoughtful analysis, see Gerald A. Heeger, "Politics in the Post-Military State: Some Reflections on the Pakistan Experience," *World Politics* 29, no. 2 (January 1977), pp. 242–62.

A second motive for intervention stems from the view held—not widely—in India that Pakistan's very existence is illegitimate, and that India has an obligation to reunite the subcontinent. Such attitudes were once quite widespread, especially in North India, but even significant conservative political elements no longer believe this to be necessary. A weak and subservient Pakistan is seen as compatible with Indian interests, and avoids the problem of incorporating millions of recalcitrant Muslims into the Indian political order, where they would again become a major political force just as they were before 1947. Even to the Hindu extremist, Indian Muslims are no threat, and, in fact, are notoriously poorly organized and led; reuniting them with their Punjabi, Pathan, and Sindhi brethren does not seem very logical. From this perspective, however, marginal adjustments in, say, Kashmir would not raise any major difficulties, and might satisfy an Indian itch to expand.

While on balance we do not think that an expansionist India (vis-à-vis Pakistan) is likely, India has substantially enhanced its capacity to expand its influence—politically and militarily. Successive Indian governments, under several different leaders, have not been reluctant to use force whenever they felt that a legitimate territorial claim was at stake, or when they felt that a show of force was useful in bargaining with a foreign adversary. While the breakup of Pakistan, encouraged and prompted by India, does not seem probable, one cannot rule out the continued expansion of Indian influence in the smaller Himalayan states and attempts to project Indian power abroad through diplomatic and military means.

To summarize, India has achieved strategic dominance over Pakistan. India has the capacity to use its armed forces to threaten Pakistan, to seize territory from it, and probably to win a decisive war. Further, India's dominance in key weapons systems, already substantial, will grow. Yet Pakistan is not without influence. As before, it can always internationalize issues such as Kashmir or the treatment of India's Muslim minority, either before a UN or an Islamic forum. It can still precipitate a war, if only to dramatize its territorial and political grievances with India; it cannot hope to win such a war, although it might manage to seize some terrain. In any case, such wars—if they again occur—are likely to remain limited in scope and duration. Neither side is really prepared for a prolonged conflict; neither side is likely to attack heavily populated areas or cities; neither side has major territorial designs on the other. What emerges, then, is an inconclusive (but not necessarily unstable) stalemate between two states with deep historical antagonisms, and yet with much to gain from cooperation.

In terms of its relations with Pakistan, the minimum tests of India's emergence as a great power would seem to be constituted by the following:
1) to maintain its military domination over Pakistan, but with an increasing reliance upon an Indian technology and resource base;
2) successfully to deter or prevent external powers from building up Pakistan's military machine to the point where it could attack India with confidence;
3) to accommodate the genuine fears and concerns of Pakistan, thus reducing Pakistan's motivation for opposing India.

With reference to the last point, such an accommodation might include a *de facto* reconciliation of the Kashmir conflict, the continued expansion of cultural, trade, and transportation links between the two countries, and the quiet but firm protection of the rights and security of India's Muslims.

Ironically, the decline in the political fortunes of the two leaders most criticized for their undemocratic practices—Indira Gandhi and Zulfikar Ali Bhutto—has also meant the disappearance of the two persons most responsible for the recent political reconciliation between India and Pakistan. Their heavy hand in domestic matters made it easier for them to negotiate with each other. It remains to be seen whether their successors, especially in Pakistan, are willing to pursue a moderate course in regional relations.

India and China

The People's Republic of China represents both a direct threat to Indian dominance of South Asia by virtue of its position in the Himalayas, and an indirect but no less potent threat to that dominance by means of its support to other regional states, especially Pakistan. China's interests in the South Asian subcontinent are limited but real. China seeks to balance Soviet influence in the region and to protect its own flank in Tibet from southern probes. India is the focus of concern on both counts: it is seen as weak, dependent, and subservient to outside patrons (the U.S. and the USSR); it also is a channel by which Chinese territorial integrity can be harmed via a threat to the line of communications through Tibet to Sinkiang, and by support of a Tibetan liberation movement. To these geostrategic interests one might add more general and symbolic concerns, such as "leadership" of the developing states and competing ideologies of development and social change.

For India, China constitutes a particularly troublesome

issue. This is in large part because China's South Asian policy is to some degree a function of Indian decisions. Had, for example, India not sought outside assistance in its encounter with China in the late 1950s, and had it been content with a lesser if not inferior position vis-à-vis China, the 1962 war might well have been averted. The commonly held belief that China soundly defeated India in their 1962 clash is perfectly correct, although the scope and intensity of that war often is misunderstood. Only limited forces were used on both sides, neither employed combat airpower (although India was sorely tempted), and no new large tracts of territory were acquired by China. The true calamity of the war for India was a failure of its leadership, civil and military, either to comprehend the intentions of the Chinese or to act effectively once these intentions became clear. In a word, panic spread throughout the political and military leadership, and it took several years for these groups to recover their nerve.[20] That the Indian Army could regenerate itself, and that Indian civilian leadership could assess and cure its own failings, were clearly demonstrated in the wars with Pakistan in 1965 and 1971, but such regenerative power is unlikely to be demonstrated against China in the near future for two interconnected reasons.

Firstly, the Sino-Indian border dispute, which had its origins in bitter territorial and ideological claims and counterclaims, has become linked to the Sino-Soviet dispute. Until there is movement in that relationship, or until India finds it possible to break away from its reliance upon the

---

20. There is a large literature on the 1962 war; for a discussion of it, see Stephen P. Cohen, "India's China War and After: A Review Article," *Journal of Asian Studies* 30, no. 4 (August 1971), pp. 847–57.

USSR for military hardware (and an increasing economic tie), there would seem to be little scope for Sino-Indian rapprochement. The exchange of ambassadors between China and India in 1976 is a start in the improvement of Sino-Indian relations, but the exchange constitutes a formal move that need not lead far in any short period of time. Secondly, China's possession of a military nuclear capability severely inhibits India's freedom of action. The Chinese nuclear force was not designed to deter or attack India, of course, but it nevertheless had a momentous impact on Indian strategic thinking. For example, in a reference to the pace of his country's nuclear development, one retired Indian brigadier recently argued that India could rely upon the tacit superpower umbrella for at least five years—or until China developed a second strike capability against the U.S. or the USSR.[21] At that point India should have its own nuclear force; in the meantime, it would need only to maintain powerful conventional forces to deal with any Chinese incursion, or seize any opportunity that may arise—e.g., a breakdown of Chinese authority in Sinkiang or Tibet.

To a world that barely remembers the war of 1962, such speculation seems bizarre. Yet India has continuously maintained between eight and ten divisions in the Himalayas, and China could bring its modest Tibetan garrison up to that strength quickly. The cost of maintaining substantial forces in the mountains is extravagant, especially for India, but its leadership is not willing or able to reach a major settlement of the border issue with China. In

---

21. Rathy Sawhny, "U.S.-Soviet-Chinese Relations: Strategic Impact on South Asia and [the] Indian Ocean," *China Report* (New Delhi) 12, no. 1 (January–February 1976), pp. 42–49.

truth, there is little incentive for either side to negotiate. China has most of the territory it needs, and has secured its routes to Sinkiang (and the frontier with the USSR). For India, no major population centers are threatened, and, above all, the tacit alliance with the USSR, referred to by Sawhny, would seem to require both a degree of Indian hostility toward China and assurance that it will not escalate too far.

A settlement of the dispute with China (which assumes that the Chinese would be willing to make concessions to India) is a possibility, but does present some grave risks. In one possible scenario, such a settlement might result in a lessening of Chinese influence in the Himalayas and a withdrawal of Chinese military support for Pakistan. This might, however, in the worst possible case, lead to a renewal of Soviet military assistance to the latter state. The status quo certainly has some drawbacks, from an Indian perspective, but such readjustments in foreign policy might decrease rather than increase security. India seems to prefer to run the risk of a two-front war with both China and Pakistan. Given China's reluctance to become involved in the conflicts of either 1965 or 1971, such a risk would seem to be minimal.

Small Powers

India's relationships with the smaller regional states (Sri Lanka, Nepal, Bhutan, and Bangladesh) impinge upon Indian strategic calculations in three ways, sometimes simultaneously.

Firstly, some of these states might be tempted to allow themselves to be used as a regional political base for an external power, or to act in concert with such a power against India. This is the Pakistani model. To date, none of these small powers has dared, although each maintains the option of doing so in that they maintain good to excellent relations with at least one of the superpowers and with China.

Secondly, and more likely, there is the possibility that any of India's smaller neighbors could deteriorate politically. Internal conflict, fragmentation, or civil war would immediately affect India in a number of ways. Such an event might lead to outside intervention by one of the superpowers or China. It might also lead to persecution of, or attacks on, minorities with ties to India (Hindus in Bangladesh, Tamils in Sri Lanka). Finally, there might develop outright collaboration with Indian dissidents. The most explosive linkages would be across the Bengal border, although the development of a pan-Bengal movement seems highly improbable.

A third linkage between India's smaller neighbors and its security is in the realm of emotion and symbolism. Involvement with such states can and has served as a testing ground for Indian diplomatic skills and ambitions. Frustrations which cannot be resolved at their source may be (temporarily) lowered by the appearance of swift and decisive action against a truculent neighbor; the recent toughness of Indira Gandhi's government toward Nepal and Bangladesh seems to be due as much to this exercise of symbolic power as to anything else.

These states together stand in much the same relationship to India, then, as India stands to the superpowers. They are too small or too weak presently to affect the military balance, yet if supported by an outside power they could become significant. They remain a testing ground for competition between India, Pakistan, and China (as India has been an area of competition between the U.S. and USSR). Their nuisance value is considerable, in part because of the presence of minority communities, but in part (again a point of comparison) because India feels some hegemonal and historic responsibility for their stability, if not also for their growth and development.

India and the Superpowers

We have discussed India's chief concern relating to superpower involvements in South Asia: that such powers refrain from actively supporting India's antagonists, especially Pakistan. And, as we have noted, much of India's diplomacy has revolved around this strategic axiom. Since 1965, India has been remarkably successful in this endeavor, as the flow of weapons to Pakistan from the United States and the Soviet Union has been reduced to an uncertain trickle.

However, two developments once again raise the question of direct Indo-superpower military entanglements, this time on the high seas. The first is the gradual increase in superpower naval units in the Indian Ocean region, and the second is the dramatic growth of the strategic importance of the Persian Gulf region since 1973. In both cases India plays a small but increasingly significant role.

For years there has been a slow increase in Soviet and American naval units operating in the Indian Ocean region.[22] The level remains small, with a permanent (but

---

22. The Indian Ocean "problem" has spawned a large literature. For a cogent survey, see W.A.C. Adie, *Oil, Politics, and Seapower: The Indian Ocean Vortex* (New York: Crane, Russak, for the National Strategy Information Center, 1975). Data on Soviet and American transits, ship-days, and types can be found in various Stockholm International Peace Research Institute (SIPRI) publications, but especially the *1975 Yearbook* (Stockholm: Almqvist & Wiksell, 1975), pp. 63–82.

tiny) U.S. force based in the Persian Gulf (since 1950), and no Soviet presence until 1967. Occasionally major fleet units of both countries transit the region, and the U.S. and USSR established modest support facilities at Diego Garcia and Berbera (Somalia), respectively. In 1971 both countries directed forces to the vicinity of the subcontinent, and the U.S. *Enterprise* and accompanying vessels sailed into the Bay of Bengal. (Circumstances for the USSR were altered more recently when Somalia expelled the Soviet Union, but the Somalia-Ethiopia conflict may well conclude with a grant by Ethiopia to the USSR of a substitute port in Ethiopian territory.)

There is some question now whether such activity could reoccur in the face of a hostile Indian Navy. Since 1971 the size of the Indian frigate, destroyer, and submarine fleet has been increased; more importantly, it has acquired some limited ship-to-ship missile capability. Any foreign navy now operating in the Indian Ocean must take this enlarged Indian capability into account, and would probably be unwilling to risk the loss of capital ships in anything less than a major conflict. Much of the discussion of the "demilitarization" of the Indian Ocean by withdrawal or control over U.S. and Soviet ships misses the point from the perspective of the states of the subcontinent: India now maintains a fleet of its own and has some limited capacity to deter seaward involvement by either superpower, thus adding to India's dominance over Pakistan.

This dominance fades when one examines a possible Indian role in the Persian Gulf. It is doubtful whether India can in the near future project its naval power that far, although its ships have made peaceful visits to Gulf ports. India would face severe problems of refueling and maintenance, as well as target acquisition, if it operated at a substantial distance from the Indian coastline. This would be particularly true if it could not act in conjunction with Iran. However, such cooperation, or an arrangement with one (or more) of the superpowers, would presumably extend the effectiveness of the Indian Navy. Lest such cooperation be thought of as fanciful, one need only be reminded of a history of external Indian military involvement under British auspices as far back as the nineteenth century, but more recently in the Gulf during both world wars, and in the Congo and Middle East under UN sponsorship in the 1950s.

CHAPTER 3
India's Nuclear Potential

No single development is likely to shape South Asia's strategic future as much as the gradual emergence of India as a nuclear power. India's 1974 "peaceful nuclear explosion" (PNE) dramatically raised the question of regional and national security to the level of an international problem. To fully comprehend the reasons for what many observers have regarded as an indefensible and malicious act, it is necessary to trace briefly the steps that led India to the "nuclear option" threshold. In doing so, we can shed light on three separate issues: the underlying motives behind the Indian nuclear program; the likely range of capabilities that the program can develop; and the strategic utility of such capabilities.

India as a Nuclear Power

India was one of the first nations to become interested in nuclear power, largely through the efforts of Homi Bhabha, an internationally recognized Indian nuclear physicist. Bhabha established a laboratory for nuclear research even before 1947, and then persuaded Jawaharlal

Nehru that nuclear energy was an area in which India could attain substantial relative advantages. Thus, by the time China exploded a nuclear device (1964), India possessed one of the world's better nuclear research and power programs, and had even exported some radioactive material. While dependent upon the United States and Canada for early reactor construction and enriched uranium fuels, India has achieved autonomy in some areas of design and construction. Thus, for India at least, "going nuclear" was not only a technical question, but also a political, moral, and economic one.

From its inception, the Indian debate over nuclear weapons reflected a variety of motives.[23] There originally was considerable uncertainty over the proper "target" for a hypothetical Indian nuclear weapon. While the public debate was triggered by the Chinese detonation of 1964, many saw the opportunity to press for a weapon which would establish Indian strategic superiority over Pakistan once and for all. Later, and more subtly, it became clear that nuclear weapons could be put to another use: as part of a more general campaign to restore India to a position of regional and global influence. This became the dominant motif in Indian strategic thinking. In this case the "target" was neither China nor Pakistan but the United States and the USSR, and the objective was not military deterrence but political influence.

As there were a variety of political and military uses

---

23. An early summary of the Indian debate is in G. G. Mirchandani, *India's Nuclear Dilemma* (New Delhi: Popular Book Service, 1968). See also K. Subrahmanyam, "India: Keeping the Option Open," in Robert M. Lawrence and Joel Larus, ed., *Nuclear Proliferation: Phase II* (Lawrence: University Press of Kansas, 1974), pp. 112–48. For a more recent comprehensive study, see Ashok Kapur, *India's Nuclear Option* (New York: Praeger, 1976).

postulated for an Indian bomb, there were a variety of economic arguments brought forward to supplement them. Proponents of the bomb claimed that it could save manpower, would not cost very much, and in the long run would be a natural complement to India's ambitious peaceful nuclear program. Critics emphasized the high cost, especially in foreign exchange, and the seeming betrayal of Gandhian inspired economic goals for the countryside. Delivery systems were singled out as a special problem, for India's missile technology has lagged far behind its nuclear program.

Finally, for a very few, the bomb was seen to have an important moral component. To right wing politicians, and to others as well, the bomb symbolized a resurgent and militant India, ready to confront its communist and Muslim enemies with the latest in technology. To the Gandhians, of course, the bomb would be anathema, although peaceful explosives were later to be accepted by some. In any case, their influence in such matters was by then minimal.

The decision to explode a PNE came in 1971 during the Bangladesh crisis. The superpowers had expressed their unwillingness to provide a nuclear umbrella to India in the 1960s, and India increasingly was resistant to paying the political price that might have accompanied public guarantees—for example, a settlement with Pakistan over the Kashmir issue, or allowing Indian territory to be used by foreign military forces. The elite consensus within India was that security problems had not eased even after the defeat of Pakistan in 1971 and that maintaining the nuclear option was vital. The PNE program was a way of demonstrating to domestic and foreign observers alike that the government still regarded security matters as important, but was not going to cross the proliferation line in an explicitly military sense.

When the explosion took place in 1974, it came as an enormous surprise, within as well as outside of India, although the decision was strongly supported by most elements within India. Many Indians, even those strongly critical of Indira Gandhi, felt that the time had come for such a demonstration of Indian capabilities, and they were proud to the point of being rhapsodic.

The policy still receives considerable support from a wide spectrum of Indian opinion, although Prime Minister Morarji Desai has gone out of his way to stress the domestic energy objective of the Government of India's nuclear policy.[24]

Some Scenarios

The above represents only the highlights of the Indian nuclear debate which flourished between 1964 and 1974. The debate was characterized by many of the same arguments that were raised in the United States, Great Britain, France, and probably the USSR and China, as each of those states "went nuclear." In the Indian situation, the

---

24. Desai repeatedly has emphasized his opposition to nuclear weapons on moral, military, and strategic grounds from virtually the first week he assumed office. It should be noted that he has not, however, permanently rejected peaceful nuclear explosions nor has he agreed to sign the Non-Proliferation Treaty. In a parliamentary statement on July 13, 1977, Desai declared that he had come to the conclusion that PNEs were not necessary, but that he would not make this commitment "for all time to come." *India News* (Washington, D.C.), July 18, 1977, p. 2.

final decision has been protracted, and is largely subservient to political and strategic calculations. The present program, therefore, represents one important option to the Indian government. It is possible that no one, not even the present leadership, knows in which direction and in what ways India will become a nuclear weapons power, or, indeed, whether it will not simply retain the "option," deferring an acquisition decision. However, we can examine these various alternative nuclear programs, noting their gains and losses from an Indian perspective, and assume that similar calculations are made in the "South Block," India's Pentagon.

Alternative One: The Status Quo

India's present course has much to recommend it. It has already yielded substantial dividends in India's relations with the superpowers, yet it is not likely to push Pakistan into a major nuclear program, nor has China become more hostile.[25] Further, maintaining the nuclear option is a low-cost strategy, and gives India's missile and electronics technologies a chance to catch up to the levels of its nuclear industry. It does not require any change in overall

---

25. This is our summary evaluation of a complex relationship. Pakistan's nuclear progress will depend on external support and its own interest in nuclear weapons; China has apparently offered no assistance in this direction, and the French have slowed down their transfer of nuclear technology to Pakistan to the point where it will be many years before the latter state can assemble anything more than a token device. As for the internal pressures for a weapon, it appears that the now-deposed Bhutto was the main advocate on behalf of the nuclear option. It is likely that Pakistan's military leaders will demand that greater efforts be made to build up depleted conventional weapons inventories before alienating major arms suppliers with a nuclear program.

conventional strategic policies, nor an expensive realignment or re-equipment of regular forces to adapt them to nuclear weapons. Finally, it enables India to maintain pressure on the signatories of the Non-Proliferation Treaty. India refuses to sign on the grounds that the nuclear powers have not been sincere about limiting their own armaments, and that were India to sign, it no longer would have the option of developing peaceful nuclear explosives.

The costs and risks of India's present nuclear strategy are minimal, and abandoning the present course is more a question of raising the stakes of the game than of being forced to abandon a position because it has become intolerable. India has suffered severe criticism from many in the West, especially those with memories of Jawaharlal Nehru's eloquent criticism of such weapons of mass destruction. Others, less concerned about India than about the proliferation process, have felt that the Western powers and the USSR should have acted to establish a nonproliferation line and turn back India's nuclear developments of potential military use; some feel that such a line still can be drawn with the application of suitable pressure on India.

From an Indian perspective, these have not been major problems. Many Indians welcome the opportunity to chip away at the misperception of their country as especially devoted to the cause of peace and nonviolence. They are more concerned about attempts to shut them off from the flow of information about nuclear technology or from the actual transfer of radioactive materials. However, their calculation is that now that India has become a nuclear power of sorts, it will have an even greater claim on the skills and resources of the advanced nuclear states, which will be reluctant to drive India into a pariah position.[26] The present nuclear option strategy is, in effect, a subtle form of blackmail, but possibly a successful one.

Alternative Two: Limited Nuclear Forces

The present Indian nuclear program could be converted into a military force. Such a force would consist of a small number of air-deliverable low-yield weapons. The economic and technological costs of this limited nuclear force are modest. What of the political and military consequences?

Such a force would give India the ability to attack any Pakistani city, and would bring several provincial Chinese population centers within destructive reach. It also would enable India to fight a limited nuclear war in the Himalayas. With the limited capacity that we have described, an Indian government might best declare that it did not regard such weapons as instruments of mass destruction, but rather as extra-powerful land mines: nuclear barricades to invasion.[27] Nevertheless, such a system

---

26. There is some division of opinion in the U.S. on the issue of letting India "get away with it"; a wide range of opinions, from bitter opposition to tacit acquiescence, was expressed during the Nuclear Regulatory Commission's hearings on the export of nuclear fuels to India held on July 20–21, 1976. The Commission, on April 20, 1978, refused (on a two to two vote) to issue a license to export 17,000 pounds of uranium to India. President Carter may—and probably will—reverse the Commission's decision, but the House and Senate may veto the President within 60 days. Even if the President's decision is left standing, the delay will cause difficulty because the uranium is needed to reload the 200,000 kilowatt nuclear power plant at Tarapur in India in 1979.

27. Several articles by Indian officers advocating tactical nuclear weapons have appeared in recent years. See, for example, Major Yogi Saksena, "A Realistic Military Strategy for India," in the *Journal of the United Services Institution of India* 104, no. 437 (October–December 1974), pp. 346–65.

would be a *military* system, and would constitute a major departure from the present program. If an Indian weapons program came *after* the announcement of, say, an Arab, Taiwanese, or Israeli system, it might have relatively little political impact on the superpowers or China. The nuclear threshold would have been breached in a major way by then, and an Indian capacity would add little to the fears of existing nuclear states. It would require some adjustment within the Indian military establishment, and might not be welcomed by the army—especially if the argument were accepted that nuclear weapons yielded "more rumble for a rupee," and manpower levels were reduced.

The likely political consequences of a limited Indian nuclear capacity are more obscure. Undoubtedly Pakistan would attempt to acquire weapons of its own, although it could not do this without outside assistance. Beyond this, the most important result of an Indian military program would be that it would constitute a *de facto* declaration of intent to acquire strategic autonomy. India would no longer need to rely upon implicit Soviet guarantees; the move thus might be welcomed by the Chinese.

Alternative Three: A Strategic Force
Were India to wait until its electronics and missile industries reached an advanced level (possibly in the mid-1980s), it could acquire an advanced nuclear capacity. Such a system would be characterized by a limited number of relatively invulnerable (or mobile) IRBM or ICBM missiles, complemented by low-technology air-deliverable weapons. India could obtain this capacity by either of the first two alternative routes: delaying a military program entirely for a number of years, or building upon a simple air-deliverable system. If India chose the first path to an

advanced program, then all of the political difficulties noted under Alternative Two would have to be faced, although India would be better protected against direct superpower or Chinese pressure. Indeed, India would have acquired the capacity to deter any outside power from deep involvement in the subcontinent and, conceivably, any other region in which it declared that it had vital interests.

While we have argued above that the calculations which might lead to an Indian nuclear capacity are primarily political, it should be noted that strategic nuclear weapons in particular have their own logic. Were India to "go nuclear," even for purely political reasons, this logic would impose itself upon the decision-makers of India, China, and the superpowers.

Assuming that adequate command-and-control procedures were instituted, a fully deployed Indian strategic missile capacity might not be disruptive. It would be "secure," in the sense that it would be used only in the case of a direct attack on India itself, and accidents would be unlikely. However, it may be beyond India's capacity to go directly to a secure, hardened (or mobile) system of strategic launch vehicles. If India opted for Alternative Two, and proceeded to slowly build a strategic capacity, there would be a considerable period in which it would be vulnerable to a first strike and could not retaliate effectively. As in other deterrent relationships, there might be pressures on either side for a preemptive attack, especially during the course of an escalating conventional war. In our judgment, such risks of an "accidental" or even planned nuclear holocaust involving India are no greater than they were during the period of greatest strategic instability in, for example, Europe; but they are no less.

Alternative Four: Encouraging Proliferation

No matter what nuclear path India takes, one more alternative is likely to open. For both political and economic gain, India might be able to exploit its own nuclear program and sell technology, training, and hardware abroad. Such a program inevitably would encourage proliferation, but this could, conceivably, become a goal of some future Indian government. It would also help defray the costs of an expanded Indian nuclear program, and would be vital in building outside political support for an independent Indian deterrent. As in the case of the second and third alternatives, a policy of encouraging proliferation implies a decision to conduct a foreign and military policy at a much higher level—even a global level—than India is operating on now. The risks are more substantial, but under certain conditions they might appear to be worthwhile to an ambitious or harassed Indian leadership.

Conclusion: The Several Uses of Nuclear Weapons

We have argued that the Indian nuclear program is largely shaped by political considerations within a context of an ever increasing technological competence. The pressures on the Indian government to expand are not overwhelming, although they do exist. An Indian nuclear military system would, as has the PNE, demonstrate to outside powers that India has joined the ranks of the powerful and is a considerable new factor in world politics. It also would demonstrate to India's own population that the government had mastered an advanced technology and was competent to manipulate the most "modern" and advanced weapons and their accompanying diplomacy: nuclear bargaining and deterrence.

While such incentives to go nuclear do exist, the future development of the Indian program is hard to predict. A rational strategy of expansion is hinted at by recent events: each stage preparing the political, psychological, and technical ground for the next. India has moved from a no-nuclear explosives status to a PNE program. It could follow this by a nuclear defense-by-denial strategy, declaring "no first use," and limiting the reach of its delivery systems to the Himalayas. This logically could be followed by a full-scale nuclear defense-by-deterrence strategy, with the formation of a second strike capability. Alternatively, an Indian leadership bent upon the creation of a full scale nuclear capacity might skip the stage of crude delivery systems, stretch out the PNE period, and go directly to a missile program. Such proliferation scenarios are easy to construct, but it would seem equally likely that the present PNE program could be indefinitely pursued with substantial political gains at a relatively low cost. It already has brought India much in the way of deference, if not respect, and it might take a severe crisis to persuade the government's leadership that the gains outweighed the obvious losses in expanding to even a limited military nuclear program. The Israeli example is partially relevant: as long as a state maintains the technical capacity to assemble a nuclear military system, and is thought to have the will to do so if pressed, it will have an effective deterrent without the full opprobrium of proliferation.

CHAPTER 4

Strategic Implications for the United States

America's Historical Involvement

Even before independence and the partition of India and Pakistan in 1947, the United States had started to play an active role in the economic and security affairs of the Indian subcontinent. Representatives of the then future Indian government appealed in 1946 for economic assistance, and both the Indian and Pakistani governments entered into discussions with Washington in 1947 concerning weapons transfers.[28] A pattern emerged at that early date relating to U.S. negotiations with India that was to become a familiar and discordant element in developing policies for the two countries. India even considered U.S. financial assistance to Pakistan an "unfriendly act." The U.S., at that stage, ultimately decided on an informal arms embargo, treating India and Pakistan alike. Such an attempt at evenhandedness did not please India. It had been suggested by India's representatives in several conversa-

---

28. United States and South Asian documents of this period are now appearing in *Foreign Relations of the United States* (FRUS). See *FRUS, 1947* III (Washington, D.C.: U.S. Government Printing Office, 1972), pp. 136 ff.

STRATEGIC IMPLICATIONS FOR THE UNITED STATES • 55

tions with American officials that the commonality of Indian and American interests should result in a special status for India in America's Asian policy. These interests included shared principles of democracy and a common concern with Soviet imperialism.[29] (It should be remembered that the two years immediately following independence were exceedingly troubled years: refugees flowed to India from Pakistan, and to Pakistan from India in numbers of about 12 million, and the winter war of 1947–48 over Kashmir between India and Pakistan exacerbated the already troubled relations between the two states. Neither country was prepared to be tolerant, and certainly not friendly, toward the other.) But America was reluctant to get deeply involved in the subcontinent. Despite some disagreement among policymakers on the point, the U.S. was willing to defer to the British the security of South Asia. This did not inhibit U.S. economic assistance of various types to both India and Pakistan, culminating later on in massive shipments of surplus agricultural products under the Public Law 480 program. American economic assistance (loans and grants) to India between 1946 and 1975 totalled $9,147 million.[30]

It was the initiation of a formal military assistance program to Pakistan in 1954 that was to shape the American role in the subcontinent for almost twenty years. Between 1954 and 1965, Pakistan received over $630 million worth of weapons as grant assistance and an additional $619 million for defense support assistance (payment of troops,

---

29. *FRUS, 1948* V (Washington, D.C.: U.S. Government Printing Office, 1975), pp. 498 ff.

30. Data from U.S. Central Intelligence Agency, *Handbook of Economic Statistics, 1976*, Research Aid, ER 76-10481, September 1976, Table 66, p. 67.

military infrastructure, etc.). Finally, Pakistan was permitted to purchase some $55 million worth of equipment on a cash or concessional basis.[31] The effect of this arms program, which was directly linked to Pakistan's entry into the Central Treaty Organization (CENTO) and the South East Asia Treaty Organization (SEATO), was to create a formidable military force in Pakistan, India's major antagonist. From the beginning of this program, Indians looked on with astonishment and anger at the arming of their prime enemy. Not until the Sino-Indian border war of 1962 did the U.S. provide military assistance to India (about $90 million in grants, primarily transportation and communications equipment, plus some $50 million worth of weapons sales), although the U.S. had earlier sold weapons to India on a cash basis, and would sell more after the Chinese attack of 1962. Both the Pakistan and India arms programs effectively ended with an arms embargo imposed after the 1965 Indo-Pakistan war, and only limited sales have been made since then. Nevertheless, the issue of arms transfers (sales, grants, and loans) remains to this day one of the key points of conflict between the U.S. and both India and Pakistan. Further, it is an issue which still may have profound domestic political consequences in South Asia.[32]

---

31. For a history of the program, see Stephen P. Cohen, "U.S. Weapons and South Asia: A Policy Analysis," *Pacific Affairs* 49, no. 1 (Spring 1976), pp. 49–69.

32. Z. A. Bhutto's inability to acquire advanced weapons from the U.S.—in large part because of his insistence upon the acquisition of a nuclear reprocessing plant which could not have yielded military benefits for at least six years—may have been a factor in the Pakistan military's calculations when they seized power in July 1977. Certainly, the Pakistani military themselves are

STRATEGIC IMPLICATIONS FOR THE UNITED STATES • 57

What were the purposes of America's economic and military involvement in the region? Briefly, South Asia was regarded as a prototypical "developing" ex-colonial region. In a broad sense, the developing and changing character of India, under an independent, democratic system of government, appealed to many American citizens and to politicians and civil servants as well. The hard work of Ambassador Chester Bowles in the early 1950s and ample publicity given to Indian aspirations by Jawaharlal Nehru combined to induce American public interest in the experiments being carried on in India. American "know how" was thought to be particularly useful to India in these early years, and a distinct aura of a "New Deal," FDR-style, for India was in the air. In a more hard-nosed sense, America's political objective with such states as India was primarily the denial of these states to any other major power which threatened U.S. interests. Since the end of World War II this meant the USSR, and later the People's Republic of China. Denial of the developing states' resources and political support to these two countries could be achieved in one of two ways: deep American involvement in the politics and security of such states, invariably topped off with a formal military tie; or, secondly, relying upon the desire for independence and autonomy of a new state to keep it free from foreign influence. It is part of the unfortunate fate of South Asia to have contained two nations which lent themselves, one each, to these two very different strategies. The dominant

---

more concerned about their deteriorating conventional weapons inventory than with the costly acquisition of an exotic and risky nuclear weapons' capability.

regional power (India) pursued a policy of autonomy and independence for itself and for the region. It is not surprising that India's smaller neighbor (Pakistan) sought external allies and contacts in the name of anti-communism, but in reality to balance the power of India. As an outside power with limited regional interests, America was soon confronted with the necessity of reconciling its desire to see strong, independent regional South Asian states, with the inescapable facts that, firstly, the states were hostile to each other, and, secondly, that supporting either—in any way—necessarily bred hostility in the other.

This fundamental strategic dilemma still haunts American relations with both Pakistan and India. The status of Indo-American relations is, to a very large extent, a function of the strategic choices made by both countries, including the United States' relations with Pakistan, and is not so much the result of a lack of understanding or sympathy or because of personality clashes. It may be true that personal, policy-specific, and intellectual conflicts have been important at certain times, but the deeper and more penetrating factor has been related to security issues. This point must be emphasized since Indo-American relations commonly have been described in terms of cyclical periods of "ups" and "downs." Such oscillations do take place, but usually because of genuine—and often irreconcilable—disagreements over strategic issues.

It is a truism, but appropriate to point out, that American interests in South Asia are characterized by diversity, diffuseness, and a high degree of indirectness. By this we mean that these interests are numerous, that they interact and influence each other to a high degree, and that they often are dependent upon extra-regional considerations. We might also add that because of their imprecise nature, there has been considerable divergence of opinion as to precisely what those interests are within the U.S. strategic community, let alone between that community and those scholars and officials who have specialized in the region. Some have emphasized anti-communism and regional stability as prime American objectives, although within this group there has been a differing emphasis on the relative importance of India or Pakistan. As time has passed, and as the global and regional variables have changed, India and Pakistan have received support from different groups in the United States. Some stress the democratic tradition of India; others view the region's rising population as a threat to all mankind (and, incidentally, welcome forced mass sterilization as a necessary evil). Finally, the specter of nuclear proliferation has brought the region to the attention of many who regard India and Pakistan, negatively, as "front line" states in this particular thrust. The U.S. debate over the range and intensity of American interests in South Asia often has been conducted in quite varying terms, and on the basis of different assumptions concerning what is important. Our own attempt at clarifying American objectives and interests is necessarily brief, but we do contend that these facts of plural interests and differing angles of vision must be recognized, as must their modest and limited importance in U.S. external policy as a whole.

U.S. Interests

There are a number of "interest clusters" embedded in American involvement in South Asia. Some of these derive from historical commitments, and are fast fading in importance, while others—such as nuclear proliferation—have only emerged in the past few years. We will examine them in terms of their relative importance to the United States and their connection with India's emergence as a dominant regional power.

As we have stated above, one of the historical reasons for American concern with South Asia lay not in the region itself, but in its relationship to the broader global balance of power. Until the mid-1960s, the balance issue remained a key factor underlying U.S. assistance both to India and to Pakistan and the U.S. attitude toward Soviet influence in these two states. The 1965 Indo-Pakistani war was a critical turning point for the U.S.; the U.S. then stood aside as the Soviets assumed the role of regional peacemaker at the Tashkent Conference in 1966. By that time, American involvements in Vietnam had deepened, and South Asia's potential for disintegration and the subcontinent's relevance to the Cold War had declined substantially. Thus, in terms of South Asia's salience to America's then accepted "vital and global interests"—developments which might directly or indirectly affect the security and welfare of the U.S. through a connection to the central U.S.-Soviet balance—India, and South Asia generally, faded rapidly as critical sectors in the mid-1960s. In recent years, South Asia has become peripherally important as European, Japanese, and American dependence upon Persian Gulf oil has increased. To the degree that, say, a war in South Asia might disrupt tanker shipments, or a hostile power might receive base or other naval facilities in the region, India and Pakistan would continue to be of strategic interest. This interest would expand were India to develop an interventionist capacity in the Gulf, or enhance its ties with important Gulf states, or perhaps if India were to engage its navy in threatening American and Soviet seapower strategies in the Indian Ocean or the Pacific.

Humanitarianism, expressed as an interest in economic development, as well as a more than casual interest in the fate of democratic forms of government in India and Pakistan, also have formed an important part of American interests in South Asia. As the revival of these issues of human rights under the Carter administration indicates, humanitarian concerns touch responsive chords with the American public. The outpouring of criticism over the Indian Emergency of 1975 was, in fact, a compliment to the people of India, as many Americans regarded India as a sister political democracy, its lack of adequate economic development notwithstanding. Here India is a special—almost unique—case for many Americans, and the Carter Administration in its attention to human rights probably is more representative of the popular mood than were either the Nixon or Ford Administrations.

A third interest, deriving from broader, global concerns, is the role of India and Pakistan in the nuclear proliferation process. Were one or both of these states to acquire a military nuclear system of substance, the U.S. would be affected in a number of ways. Firstly, this development would again breach the symbolic barrier between peaceful and military nuclear technology. With the partial exception of France, all earlier powers had weapons as their first objective.[33] Critics of proliferation stress the importance of demonstrating that the non-military route of nuclear de-

---

33. Lawrence Scheinman emphasizes the ambiguous character of the French nuclear program, which in this way was a precursor of India's. See *Atomic Energy Policy in France under the Fourth Republic* (Princeton: Princeton University Press, 1965).

velopment is just as dangerous as the military route, and thus should be seen as politically unviable in the Indian setting. A limited Indian military nuclear system, *per se*, need not threaten the U.S., although it might be useable against a facility such as Diego Garcia or a hostile American fleet, and thus serve some deterrent function. The prospect does, however, raise the risk of regional nuclear war, possibly making such a war more likely elsewhere, and possibly stimulating the emergence of a proliferation chain either through emulation or direct assistance.[34]

Obviously India itself would not profit if nuclear acquisition were to lead in such directions; there is a shared interest between India and the U.S., as well as other nuclear powers, on this point. Were India to go nuclear, it presumably would want to do so in a way that kept Pakistan from doing so and that did not raise Chinese fears unduly. It may well be that this would be difficult, if not impossible, to achieve, and that India's true interests lie in maintaining its dominant conventional military superiority, rather than changing the ground rules to a nuclear balance which might permit Pakistan once again to claim the necessity of equality between the two states.

There are few ties between the United States and the states of South Asia that impinge directly upon the security or prosperity of the United States. The ties that do exist are intangible and lie more in the realm of emotion, but are no less real or important to those who hold them. Chief among these is the dependency relationship which grew between Pakistan and the U.S. For many years Pakistan deliberately subordinated its political autonomy

---

34. See Lewis A. Dunn and Herman Kahn, *Trends in Nuclear Proliferation* (Hudson Institute, HI-2336/3-RR, May 15, 1976).

for the sake of its American ally, and eagerly collaborated on a number of joint security and military arrangements, some of which were highly sensitive. Other than material dependency, there also grew a sense of political and psychological dependency, and an assumption that Pakistan had a legitimate claim on American resources and military technology. The repeated refusal to sell high performance weapons to Pakistan since 1967 (e.g., most recently, the Carter administration's refusal to sell A-7 attack aircraft), has left Pakistan without a strong and reliable external source of military equipment. The withdrawal of American support for Pakistan was not expected to lead to an expanded set of U.S. involvements with India, which had its own reliable sources of military hardware, but the decline in U.S.–Pakistani relations has considerably improved political ties between the United States and India.

If American ties with Pakistan have been characterized by a concern with the security and autonomy of a long-time (although rapidly fading) ally, those with India are considerably more diverse. India's democratic traditions, its economic development, cultural and academic relations, and easy access for American business, cultural, and academic groups, all have been important assets for a large number of Americans.

American Policy

American policy toward South Asia, more particularly India, is not made by a single individual or even by a single branch of government. It is now, as in the past, the sometimes unpredictable outcome of a process of bargaining within and between branches of government, reflecting somewhat different interests and approaches, with sporadic intervention by both Congress and the President.[35] However, two broad perspectives or approaches to America's South Asia policy have contended for dominance over the past twenty-five years. One emphasized India's (and South Asia's) role in the global balance of power, particularly with regard to the United States' effort to contain and meet Soviet and Chinese influences in the so-called rimland states. At times this strategy has meant the encouragement of Asian autonomy and independence, while in an earlier period it had meant the subordination of Asian concerns (and even American interests in Asia) to the interests of major allies, especially the former European colonial states. This strategy also has implied a lack of interest in domestic political structures in the South Asian states, unless it was thought that a particular political system implied support for broader American positions, or that political instability weakened a state's capacity to serve as a buffer or resisting force to communist influence. We label this approach the "global" perspective; it clearly has dominated American policy-making toward South Asia for many years.

A second approach, however, has been profoundly influential, if not on the strategic then at least on the tactical level. This approach, which we term "regional," does not deny the importance of the global struggle for influence nor even the role of the South Asian states in that struggle.

---

[35]. See the various case studies, as well as the introductory chapter by Lloyd and Susanne Rudolph in their edited collection, *The Coordination of Complexity in South Asia: Papers Prepared for the Conduct of Foreign Policy* VII, Appendix V (Washington, D.C.: U.S. Government Printing Office, 1975).

It places regional matters at the top of the political agenda, however, and assumes that global strategic interests can best be served by more mundane, limited objectives and programs. Perhaps naively, this approach argues the realism of idealism, especially with regard to India, and stresses the limits of direct American influence in that vast and complicated nation. In brief, the approach argues that attempts to play the "great game" of diplomatic maneuvering in South Asia have met with limited success at best. True, Pakistan was a loyal and useful ally for a number of years, but the U.S. has long since demonstrated that it is unwilling to maintain that alliance, nor does it now gain very much by it. Pakistan's last useful service was performed when it helped manage the early stages of the Sino-American detente; with Americans talking directly to both Russians and Chinese, Pakistan's once unique role of diplomatic intervention is of less or no importance now. Nixon, Kissinger, and Ford all clearly felt a sense of obligation to Pakistan, but not so much that they were willing to suspend the "one time exception" sale of weapons to Pakistan, to commit American forces in defense of East Bengal in 1971, or to sell aircraft without a Pakistani pledge to forego nuclear reprocessing in its negotiations with France. Pakistan's current position in the U.S. is even more bleak, as further negotiations for A-7 aircraft have led to an outright American refusal. Thus, Pakistan is a minor factor in regional relations—and struggling for its survival—and India is no more willing to serve as an instrument of American policy now than when it was more vulnerable to outside pressure and internal disorder. In fact, the departure of Pakistan from CENTO, and its corollary, the development of closer Pakistan-Soviet ties, would seem to be a logical next phase in the evolution of its policy, but such a move would be a "non-event" as far as the U.S. is concerned.

In our opinion, there must be a search for an alternative to the application of global and balance of power criteria to South Asia, emphasizing a reconsideration of the region as a whole and India's role in it. Without according India an absolutely free hand in its regional relations, India nevertheless cannot be challenged effectively there, at least by the U.S. Further, there is no need for such a challenge. Even an "imperial" India expanding into the Himalayan states, Bangladesh, and Pakistan would not threaten any important American interests, although it would most assuredly threaten Indian ones. A sober Indian leadership will realize this. Beyond India's obvious regional influence, India seeks a broader role, and this also is not incompatible with American interests. As one of the most experienced and mature of the nonaligned states, India plays an important function in both UN and nonaligned forums, and a symbolic affirmation of that importance would not be inappropriate.[36]

One prescription, therefore, is for a continuation of the process in accommodating Indian interests and objectives which began as far back as 1967 when the U.S. adopted a policy that drastically cut the flow of weapons to Pakistan, and was again stated publicly, although quietly, in 1972.

We also believe that there is a growing compatibility between America's global, strategic interests and its historic regional concerns in South Asia. Until the late 1960s, there was an obvious discontinuity between American

---

36. Making India a permanent member of the Security Council, and perhaps adding other states to that body, has been suggested, but this would require Charter revision and undoubtedly would induce heated debate.

support for Pakistan—a support useful for the broader strategic balance—and attempts to forge a sound political relationship with India. A strategically sound U.S. policy for South Asia based on Pakistan never could be balanced, even by liberal economic assistance, and some came to the bizarre conclusion that America's true objective was to cripple and neutralize Indian power.[37] With the decline in Pakistan's role as an intermediary among the great powers—although not its decline in importance, for it is forging a new role as an ancillary Middle Eastern power—direct American military support is no longer necessary, and U.S.-Indian relations have become normal.

Several cautions are in order. Despite the sharing of a democratic form of government, and despite some common economic and even strategic interests, the prospects for a strong and fully cordial U.S.-India relationship must be viewed with skepticism. A number of important issues may be expected to continue to divide the two states: India's refusal to forego an uninspected nuclear industry; the American presence in the Indian Ocean; a residual but real American concern over the stability and security of Pakistan; and quite different perspectives on the proper organization of the international economic order. Each of these issues is negotiable, but each one could lead to serious disagreements. All of the goodwill in the world, and all of the scholarly and cultural exchange programs that can be devised, will not be sufficient to prevent future serious disagreements between the two states. And, for a

---

37. Suggested by Baldev Raj Nayar, "Treat India Seriously," *Foreign Policy* 18 (Spring 1975), pp. 133–54. Also instructive are the comments by William Barnds and W. Howard Wriggins, and Nayar's rejoinder, in *Foreign Policy* 20 (Fall 1975), pp. 250–53.

variety of motives, there are individuals and groups within each state eager to criticize the other or to force a break between them.

Finally, in a world characterized by growing multipolarity, it may not be in the strategic interest of either state to work toward a formalization of "cordial" relations. India, especially, cannot afford to be taken for granted and must maintain a creative tension in its relations with *both* superpowers, balancing each against the other. (This is one reason that it may be expected that India will do its utmost to improve relations with China, even while retaining good working accords with the USSR.) Nor is it likely that the U.S. would wish to become identified in South Asia as an outright supporter of India. Pakistan retains some marginal utility for the U.S. and a strategy of minimal involvement also means that losses are likely to be minimal as well. Furthermore, even smaller states such as Nepal, Bhutan, Bangladesh, and Sri Lanka would not appreciate an American policy that unqualifiedly rested upon a recognition of India's hegemony in the region. That India now holds regional dominance nevertheless is the starting point for any rational U.S. policy for the 1980s.

Addendum: The View from Moscow

If, as is almost certainly so, the United States continues to refrain from a major rearmament of Pakistan—and if India's strategic autonomy grows, coupled with closer Indo-Chinese ties, hence lessening the nuclear threat—then the Soviet Union may reconsider its own South Asian policy. From the Russian perspective, India has been a useful ally in the subcontinent, but one that has declined in importance since 1971. Firstly, India no longer is dependent upon the Soviet Union for arms to deal with Pakistan itself, and India has expressed a desire to diversify its arms sources.[38] Secondly, a series of small but significant diplomatic arrangements with the People's Republic of China indicate a growing and apparently mutual desire to normalize relations between the two states.[39] Thus, India is neither as reliant upon the USSR as it used to be nor is it as likely to be as useful to the USSR in the Sino-Soviet dispute.

The American refusal to sell advanced weapons to Pakistan, let alone to supply them on a grant basis, provides a golden opportunity for the Soviet Union. In 1968 the Russians did supply some weapons to Pakistan, primarily to induce that state to reconcile its differences with India and present a common front to China. The same motive still exists. With the decline in Chinese military support to Pakistan, the Russians have an opportunity to "rescue" a state let down both by the Chinese and the Americans, as well as to chasten an increasingly indepen-

---

38. Recent Indian discussions of acquisition of a so-called DPSA (Deep Penetration Strike Aircraft) have stressed that India's policy "has been and continues to be" dependent upon a variety of sources for "equipment and know how." Unless outside assistance can be obtained for upgrading the Indian-manufactured HF-24, the choice seems to be between the Viggen, Mirage, and Jaguar, all European aircraft, possibly to be built under license. *The Hindu* (Madras), October 19, 25, 1977.

39. Indian officials explain that their strategy is to normalize relations with China without raising the "territorial question." *The Hindu* (Madras), October 16, 1977. Many Indians have gone further and suggested that India give up claims on strategically worthless territory. For a soldier's perspective, with this conclusion, see Major-General A. M. Vohra, "China's Strategic Posture in the 1980s," United Service Institution of India, *Paper Number One*, February 1972, p. 23.

dent India. In fact, from the Russian perspective, Pakistan may become a better ally than India: it has stronger ties to the Persian Gulf and the Middle East, and is far more desperate for modern, effective weapons.

In terms of strict calculations of power politics, it is not farfetched speculation to predict the emergence of a Soviet-supported Pakistan; the main obstacle would seem to be not strategic, but the antipathy of many groups in Pakistan (as well as some of its Arab supporters) to communism and to the Soviet Union itself. The outcomes of political arrangements in Pakistan over the next year or two would appear to be critical concerning future Soviet-Pakistani relationships.

CHAPTER 5

General Conclusions

Two questions were posed at the outset of this study. First: "Is India an emergent power—in effect, a country of substantial strategic importance now, and of even greater potential importance?" We believe that the evidence presented in the previous chapters supports an affirmative answer. India has achieved hegemony in a region which —while not of critical importance to so-called vital U.S. interests—is of concern to many Americans for strategic, political, economic, and humanitarian reasons. Further, Indian dominance in South Asia leads one to give greater weight to its potential involvement in neighboring regions, as well as to its role as an intermediary in the North-South dialogue.

The data are abundant to underscore the growing strength of the military power of India, including potential nuclear capacities, and the increasing willingness of both civilian and military leaders to harness this power effectively in the interests of India's regional hegemony. Traditional subcontinental and border rivalries, especially with Pakistan and China, remain active, but Pakistan now is developing closer ties with Iran, Turkey, and the Arab world, with possible stronger links with the USSR to be forged in the future; India, in turn, is in the process of negotiating improved accords with the People's Republic of China. Overall, subcontinental disputes are declining in intensity, in part because of a recognition of India's standing of dominance. While we cannot be certain that India's strength can be sustained in other than regional terms, this is in itself sufficiently important to warrant application of the "great power" label.

Any such categorization is, of course, merely a crude simplifying device. It must not obscure the contingencies which accompany the growth of India's prestige and power. The region contains numerous sources of instability and potential conflict within its states, between them, and as parties at dispute with external powers. Questions of conventional and nuclear security, Kashmir and other territorial and resource disputes, as well as communal fears, are unresolved sources of conflict between India and one or more of its neighbors, including China. Internal problems of political stability, economic development, population growth, and political upheavals following legislated measures of social change will continue into the future. Regional economic indicators, despite some recent favorable trends in agriculture and trade, are not encouraging. It is our estimation, however, that India is reasonably well equipped to deal with most of these problems (many of which constitute the daily fare of Indian political and administrative life). And, as a measure of the intent and purpose of its leadership, India has pursued the objective of national power and prestige in the face of considerable foreign criticism and domestic disruption for a number of years. There is no reason to believe that such a leadership perspective will fade in the future.

The second question posed in Chapter 1 was: "If so,"—

if India does approach great power status—"what are the policy implications for the United States?" Our conclusions and future speculations have been presented in Chapter 4. At the minimum the United States can and should do nothing to challenge India's regional leadership. This does not imply the abandonment of equally legitimate (although perhaps less important) U.S. interests embedded in its relationships with other regional states. A prudent diplomacy will recognize that Indo-American ties for the forseeable future will involve tensions over issues in regional and global affairs—economic justice, weapons proliferation, nuclear technology—that are based on differences in perception and interest.

At the maximum, the U.S. must consider the alternative of actively sustaining India's regional leadership—although again, the legitimate ambitions and goals of other regional states need not be ignored. As we have stated above, a wise Indian leadership will recognize that America's concern for India's neighbors does not represent—and for many years has not represented—an attempt at containment or harassment. Such an activist diplomacy also will identify many areas of mutual cooperation and support. It also will foster the political mechanisms which allow each state to represent its interests and objectives to the other effectively.

What are the mechanisms for exploring a new and untested relationship between the United States and India? As American interests in India and the region are pluralist and diverse, so should there be an opportunity for contact between American and Indian businessmen, scholars, intellectuals, and others. To a considerable degree, the various commissions, exchange programs, state visits, and other forms of public diplomacy have provided the channels for contact at several levels between Indians and Americans, although some of these contacts have produced conflict and dissension as well. Yet, such forums, however necessary and useful, can only be adjuncts to the development of a sustained and intelligent dialogue on a number of conflict-laden issues. For this dialogue to occur, the emerging importance of India in regional and world politics must be more broadly recognized in the United States and elsewhere. The tragic alternative will be the growth of a new center of power and influence—which we believe has already occurred—whose contribution to the solution of some of the most critical global issues of our time will be neither understood nor encouraged.

Appendices and Bibliographical Note

APPENDIX A: INDIA IN COMPARATIVE PERSPECTIVE
A-1 Relative Burden of Military Expenditures   77
A-2 Comparative Force Levels: Selected Asian States   78
A-3 Defense Spending, Population, Economy   79

APPENDIX B: INDIAN DEFENSE PRODUCTION
B-1 Weapons Produced Under License in India, 1974   80
B-2 Indigenously Designed Weapons, 1975   82

APPENDIX C: WEAPONS AND FORCE INVENTORY
C-1 Indian Weapons and Force Inventory   84

BIBLIOGRAPHICAL NOTE   87

Appendix A-1: Relative Burden of Military Expenditures*

Military Expenditure (as % of GNP)	Per Capita GNP (in dollars)					
	Less than $100	Between 100–199	Between 200–299	Between 300–499	Between 500–999	1,000–1,999	above 2,000
More than 10%	North-Vietnam		Egypt	North Korea Jordan Syria	Iran Iraq	Saudi Arabia	USSR
5–10		Pakistan	PRC Nigeria		(Taiwan) ROC Mongolia	Portugal	Germany (GDR) U.S. Gt. Britain
2–4.9	Burma	India Indo-nesia	Thailand	South Korea	Brazil Turkey		Germany (FRG) France Sweden
1–1.9	Afghanistan		Philippines				Switzerland
1	Bangladesh Nepal		Sri Lanka		Mexico		Japan

*1974 data derived from Arms Control and Disarmament Agency, *World Military Expenditures and Arms Transfers, 1965–74* (Washington: U.S. Government Printing Office, 1976), p. 6.

Appendix A-2: Comparative Force Levels: Selected Asian States*

	# Equivalent Infantry Divisions	# Armored Divisions	# Heavy, Medium Tanks	# Combat Aircraft	# Submarines	# Major Surface Vessels
China	128	10	7,000	4,250	56	32
India	27	4	1,880	950	8	32
Iran	4	4	1,360	317	(3 on order)	11 (6 on order)
Japan	12	1	600	448	16	47
Indonesia	4	.3		30	3	10
Pakistan	14	2.6	1,000	217	3	8

*Derived from individual country entries in *The Military Balance, 1976–77*, International Institute for Strategic Studies. Light tanks and APCs are excluded, as are patrol vessels.

Appendix A-3: Defense Spending, Population, Economy*

	Population (1,000)	GNP (bn. US $)	Milex (bn. US $)	Armed Forces Manpower (1,000)	Percent GNP Spent on Defense (C/B)	Milex† per capita	Milex Manpower	# Civilians per soldier	Percent men 18–45 (in Mil.)
China	850–900,000	$245.0	$17.0	3,525	6.9%	$19	$4,822	247	2%
India	610,930	89.7	2.8	1,055	3.1	5	2,664	578	.8
Iran	33,810	56.8	9.5	300	16.7	288	31,666	112	4.6
Japan	112,540	502.5	5.0	235	1	45	21,523	479	.9
Indonesia	133,110	29.2	1.1	246	3.8	8	4,471	541	1
Pakistan	72,790	10.1	.807	428	8	11	1,886	170	4.1

*All data are 1974–76, and derived from *The Military Balance, 1976–77*, International Institute for Strategic Studies. Certain figures are estimates (e.g., China's population, and economy); others are not exactly comparable because of different measurement techniques.
†Milex = Military Expenditures

Appendix B-1: Weapons Produced Under License in India, 1974*

Licenser	Designation, Description	Power plant	Armament	Date of License	Entered production	Indigenous percent
Czechoslovakia	OT-62 APC			1970		
France	HAL SA-315 Cheetah high altitude helicopter (Aerospatiale SA-315 Lama)	T(l:Fr.)		Sept. 1970	1972	Phase 1: assembly from imported components
	HAL Alouette III helicopter	T(l:Fr.)		1962	1965	Manuf. from local raw materials
	Bharat SS-11 ATM	S	Warhead: HE	1970	1971	100
	Type A69 Avisos frigate	D(l:Fr.)	Exocet SSM (l:Fr.); ASW;RL; TT	Feb. 1974	First to be laid down mid-1975	
U.K.	HAL AJIT light weight fighter (Gnat Mark II)	J(L:UK)	Aden cannon (l:UK)	1973	1976	90 Indian R&D
	HAL HS-748 transport	J(L:UK)			1959	Assembly from imported kit
	Vijayanta medium battle tank	D(l:UK)	105mm guns	1965	1967	80
	"Leander" class ASW frigate	Turbine (l:UK)	1 Wasp hel.	1965	Launch dates:	First: 53

				(I:UK); 2 Seacat SAM launchers (I:UK); ASW	Oct. 1968 May. 1970 Oct. 1972 Mar. 1974	
USSR	HAL MiG-21 FL fighter Mach 2.0	J(L:USSR)	Atoll AAM (L:USSR)	1964	1966	80
	HAL MiG-21 M fighter Mach 2.0	J(L:USSR)	Atoll AAM (L:USSR)	1970	1973	60
	HAL MiG-21 FMA multi-role version	J(L:USSR)		1974	1975	Assembly of 23 from knocked-down parts
	Bharat K-13A Atoll AAM	S	Warhead: HE	1964	1970	

Abbreviations:

AAM = Air to Air Missile
APC = Armored Personnel Carrier
ASW = Anti-Submarine Warfare
ATM = Anti-Tank Missile
D   = Diesel
HAL = Hindustan Aeronautics Ltd.
HE   = High Explosive
hel = Helicopter

I   = Imported
J   = Jet
L   = Licence
S   = Solid propellant
SAM = Ship to Air Missile
SSM = Ship to Ship Missile
T   = Turboshaft

*Source: Stockholm International Peace Research Institute, *World Armaments and Disarmament: Yearbook 1975* (Stockholm: Almqvist and Wiksell, 1975), Appendix 8A, p. 208.

Appendix B-2: Indigenously Designed Weapons in Development or Production in India, 1975*

Designation, description	Power plant	Armament	Date design begun	Date in production	Production rate	Status of program: other information
HAL HJT-16 MkI Kiran jet trainer	J(l:UK)	7.62mm MG rockets	1961	1968	25/year	Total AF/Navy req: 180
HAL HJT-16 MkII Kiran COIN/ground attack vers	J(L:UK)		1974			Under development
HAL HF-24 Marut MkI light fighter bomber	J(L:UK)	Aden guns (UK); rockets; bombs	1956	1963		Doubtful whether more than 125 single seaters will be produced
HAL HF-24 Marut MkIT tandem trainer vers	J(L:UK)	Aden guns (UK); rockets; bombs	1967	1974		AF req: 10; production will close by end of 1976 with delivery of last MkIT trainer
HAL HF-24 Marut Mk2	J(UK Fr.)		1969	Test flight 1972		4 pre-production planes ordered; AF prefers HF-73 Marut Mk3 and HF-24 Mk2 probably cancelled
HAL HF-73 deep-penetration strike fighter (HAL-24 Mk3 derivative)	J(UK)		1969	Prototype flight 1980		Design studies completed; progress slow, further development not yet financed
HAL HAC-33 light STOL transport	T(UK)		Design completed 1974			AF and Navy req: "large number"

HAL HPT-32 basic trainer	P(U.S.)	Design completed 1974	Scheduled to replace AF HT-2 from 1981–82
Ship to ship missile			Test completed Dec.1975; no further details available
Main battle tank		1970	1980	Design: Avadi R&D Dept
APC		Prototype trials 1973	Large-scale production shortly
Corvette-type patrol boat		1974	Planning
Nuclear-powered submarine	N	1974	Design to be completed 1980	Planning; no details released
Aeroengines		1965	HAL, Bangalore, R&D
Electronics		1956	Bharat Electronics; HAL Lucknow; avionics
Small arms		1962	India nearly self-sufficient in smallarms
Target drones		1970	Testing: July 1974; speed: Mk 1.4
Unguided rockets			

Abbreviations: APC—Armored Personnel Carrier; COIN—Counterinsurgency; HAL—Hindustan Aeronautics Ltd.; I—Imported; J—Jet; L—License; MG—Machine gun; N—Nuclear; P—Piston; T—Turboprop

*Source: Stockholm International Peace Research Institute, *World Armaments and Disarmament: Yearbook 1976* (Stockholm: Almqvist and Wiksell, 1976), Appendix 6E, p. 234.

Appendix C-1: Indian Weapons and Force Inventory*

Army:

Officers and men: 913,000 [est. 180,000 additional in various para-military formations, Border Security Force, generally trained and equipped as light infantry]; 2 armored divisions; 5 independent armored brigades [equivalent of at least two armored divisions]; 15 infantry divisions; 10 mountain divisions [distributed along the Himalayan and Kashmir borders]; 6 independent infantry brigades; 1 parachute brigade; 9 independent artillery brigades (incl. about 20 AA arty regiments), plus air observation squadrons.

Medium tanks: 180 *Centurion* Mk. 5/7 [U.K.], 1,000 T-54/-55 [USSR], some 700 *Vijayanta* [Indian mfd. under U.K. license]

Light tanks: 150 PT-76 [USSR]

Armored Personnel Carriers: 700 OT-62/-64(2A) and Mk. 2/4A [now Indian mfd. under Czech license]

Artillery: about 2,000 75mm, 76mm and 25-pdr (mostly towed), about 300 100mm, 105mm (incl. pack howitzer) and *Abbott* 105mm sp [U.K.], 550 130 mm [USSR] and 5.5 in. [UK] guns and how.; 500 120mm, 160mm mortars; 57mm, 106mm recoilless rifles; SS-11 and ENTAC ATGW; 100mm ATk guns; 30mm, 40mm AA guns; 40 *Tigercat* SAM.

Navy:

Officers and men: 42,500 including Naval Air; 8 submarines (Soviet F-class); 1 aircraft carrier [I.N.S.

Vikrant], capacity 25 aircraft, incl. 18 *Sea Hawk*, 4 *Alize*, 2 *Alouette* III hel.; 2 cruisers [both obsolete, I.N.S. *Mysore*, I.N.S. *Delhi*]; 3 destroyers; 26 frigates (3 *Leander*-class with 2 *Seacat* SAM, 10 *Petya* class [USSR]; 9 general purpose, 1 AA, 3 training: 8 *Osa*-class (fast patrol boat) with *Styx* ship-to-ship missile (8 more on order) [Styx weighs 1.2 tons and has a 12-18 mile range]; 15 patrol boats (14 coastal, incl. 5 *Poluchat*-class); 8 minesweepers (4 inshore): 1 landing ship, 6 landing craft (5 *Polnocny*-class).

Naval Air Force:

1 attack sqn. with 25 *Sea Hawk* (10 in carrier)
1 Maritime recon. sqn. with 12 *Alize* (4 in carrier)
1 Maritime recon. sqn. with 3 *Super Constellation*, 3 Ilyushin-38
2 hel. sqns. with 22 *Alouette* III
2 ASW sqns. with 12 *Sea King* hel.
22 miscell. training and utility aircraft

Air Force:

Officers and men: 100,000; 3 lt. bbr. sqns. with 80 Canberra B(I) 58, B(I)12; 13 Fighter (ground attack) sqns.: 5 with 130 Sukhoi-7B, 3 with 80 HF-24; *Marut* IA, 5 with 130 *Hunter* F56; 11 interceptor sqns. with 275 MiG-21 PFMA/FL/MF; 8 interceptor sqns. with 250 *Gnat* Mk. 1.: 1. recon. sqn. with 12 Canberra PR57: 14 transport sqns. with 12 I1.-14, 28 HS-748, 3 Tu-124, 40 C-119G, 30 An-12; 29 *Otter*, 40 C-47, 21 *Caribou*; 12 Hel. sqns. with 100 Mi-4, 35-Mi 8; 120 *Chetak* (*Alouette* III mfd. India), 12AB-47; 20 SAM sites with 120 SA-2.

On order: 110 MiG-21 MF, 100 *Ajeet* [high performance *Gnat*], 10 HS-748, 55 *Marut*, 90 *Iskra*.

*Source: All figures derived from International Institute for Strategic Studies, *The Military Balance*, 1976–77; comments in brackets are the authors'.

Bibliographical Note

This monograph, brief as it is, touches upon a number of different political and strategic problems. The following discussion of the relevant literature is by no means inclusive, but is intended as a descriptive guide for further reading and study.

The subject of "great powers" is covered in one way or another in all of the international relations literature, but several recent books attempt useful approaches. Of special value are Raymond Aron's classic *Peace and War: A Theory of International Relations* (New York: Praeger, 1968), and a more specialized study by Steven L. Spiegel, *Dominance and Diversity: The International Hierarchy* (Boston: Little, Brown, 1972). Two books that attempt quantitative measures of the interrelationship between military, economic, and political power are Michael D. Wallace, *War and Rank Among Nations* (Lexington: Lexington Books, 1973), and Emile Benoit, *Defense and Economic Growth in Developing Countries* (Lexington: Lexington Books, 1973).

A few of the better introductions to contemporary Indian politics are: Robert L. Hardgrave, Jr., *India: Government and Politics in a Developing Nation*, 2nd ed. (New York:

Harcourt, Brace, Jovanovich, 1975); Henry C. Hart, ed., *Indira Gandhi's India: A Political System Reappraised* (Boulder: Westview Press, 1976); and Rajni Kothari, *Politics in India* (Boston: Little, Brown, 1970).

There are a number of excellent studies of Indian foreign and defense policies, but no definitive account has yet appeared. Of the major surveys, mention should be made of William J. Barnds, *India, Pakistan and the Great Powers* (New York: Praeger, 1972) and G. W. Choudhury, *India, Pakistan, Bangladesh, and the Major Powers* (New York: Free Press, 1975); Barnds and Choudhury wrote their studies after leaving the U.S. and Pakistani governments, respectively. There is no equivalent book by an Indian, but Nehru's own writings and speeches may still be read with profit. Nehru's long-time associate and friend, V. K. Krishna Menon, is well represented by Michael Brecher's *India and World Politics: Krishna Menon's View of the World* (New York: Praeger, 1968). The subject of nonalignment is skillfully reexamined by A. P. Rana, *The Imperatives of Nonalignment* (New Delhi: Macmillan, 1976). Perhaps the best single short summary of Indian foreign policy is Leo E. Rose's chapter, "The Foreign Policy of India," in James N. Rosenau, Kenneth Thompson, and Gavin Boyd, eds., *World Politics* (New York: Free Press, 1976). William J. Barnds' regional chapter, "South Asia," in the same volume, is equally lucid and insightful. See also Richard L. Park, "India's Foreign Policy," in *Foreign Policy in World Politics*, 5th ed., edited by Roy C. Macridis (Englewood Cliffs: Prentice-Hall, 1976). The authoritative Indian account of the Kashmir conflict is in Sisir Gupta's massive *Kashmir: A Study in India–Pakistan Relations* (Bombay and New York: Asia Publishing House, 1966).

Pakistan's foreign policy was skillfully articulated by

Field-Marshal Muhammad Ayub Khan in his *Friends Not Masters: A Political Autobiography* (New York: Oxford, 1967), and much of Z. A. Bhutto's exuberance and ambition emerges in his manifesto, *The Myth of Independence* (London: Oxford University Press, 1969).

The defense establishments of India and Pakistan now are receiving the scrutiny they deserve by both foreign and regional scholars. Basic sources include the quarterly *Journal* of the United Services Institution of India (now over 110 years old) and the various publications of the Indian Institute for Defence Studies and Analyses (New Delhi). A new publication in Pakistan, *Defense Journal* (Karachi) also is worth examination. More general Indian publications include *Seminar, International Studies,* and *India Quarterly,* all published in New Delhi. A full-length and detailed study of the Pakistan military now is available in Hasan Askari Rizvi, *The Military and Politics in Pakistan* (Lahore: Progressive, 1974), which supplements Major-General Fazal Muqeem Khan, *The Story of the Pakistan Army* (Karachi: Oxford University Press, 1963). An insightful history of the Indian Army is found in Philip Mason, *A Matter of Honour: An Account of the Indian Army, Its Officers and Men* (New York: Holt, Rinehart, 1974), while a more analytic approach is in Stephen P. Cohen, *The Indian Army: Its Contribution to the Development of a Nation* (Berkeley: University of California Press, 1971).

Of the studies of contemporary defense policy, the work of K. Subrahmanyam is among the most stimulating and informative. A collection of his papers can be found in *Perspectives in Defence Planning* (New Delhi: Abhinav Publications, 1972). An even more hawkish study is by Rohit Handa, *Policy for India's Defence* (New Delhi: Chetana, 1976). An earlier but still valuable book is Lorne J. Kavic,

India's Quest for Security: Defense Policy, 1947–1965 (Berkeley: University of California Press, 1967).

India's wars have generated a large literature and a few outstanding books. Several derive from the 1962 conflict. Brig. John (J.P.) Dalvi's *Himalayan Blunder: The Curtain-raiser to the Sino-Indian War of 1962* (Bombay: Thacker, 1969) represents the views of many of the field grade officers who actually saw combat (Dalvi was himself captured); Dalvi's book was written in response to the self-exculpatory account by Lt. Gen. Brij Mohan Kaul, *The Untold Story* (Bombay: Allied Publishers, 1967). Only slightly more reliable is Neville Maxwell's devastating *India's China War* (London: Jonathan Cape, 1970), which relies heavily on secret Indian sources, to the sorrow of those who assisted him. Allen S. Whiting's careful study of Chinese policy is far more believable. See the relevant chapters in *The Chinese Calculus of Deterrence: India and Indonesia* (Ann Arbor: University of Michigan Press, 1975). The 1965 Indo-Pakistan war was inconclusive, and both sides claimed victory. However, the results of the 1971 conflict were more clear-cut. One of the most interesting studies is Mohammed Ayoob and K. Subrahmanyam, *The Liberation War* (New Delhi: S. Chand, 1972). An excellent overview of the conflict is Robert V. Jackson, *South Asia Crisis, India, Pakistan, and Bangladesh: A Political and Historical Analysis of the 1971 War* (London: Chatto & Windus, 1975).

The Indian Ocean has emerged as an area of interest for many scholars, well represented in Alvin J. Cottrell and R. M. Burrell, *The Indian Ocean: Its Political, Economic, and Military Importance* (New York: Praeger, 1972). W. A. C. Adie, *Oil, Politics, and Seapower: The Indian Ocean Vortex* (New York: Crane, Russak, for the National Strategy Information Center, 1975), is a useful recent summary.

BIBLIOGRAPHICAL NOTE · 91

The issue of nuclear proliferation has generated a large literature, and there have been several studies of India. Ashok Kapur, *India's Nuclear Option* (New York: Praeger, 1976) takes a sympathetic approach, and the chapter of Onkar Marwah in Marwah and Ann Shulz, eds., *Nuclear Proliferation and the Near-Nuclear Countries* (Cambridge: Ballinger, 1975) is excellent. An introduction to the general problem of proliferation can be found in Robert M. Lawrence and Joel Larus, eds., *Nuclear Proliferation: Phase II* (Lawrence: University Press of Kansas, for the National Security Education Program, 1974), which has a chapter on India by K. Subrahmanyam; and in Ted Greenwood, Harold A. Feiveson, and Theodore B. Taylor, *Nuclear Proliferation* (New York: McGraw-Hill, for the Council on Foreign Relations, 1977).

National Strategy Information Center, Inc.

STRATEGY PAPERS

India: Emergent Power? by Stephen P. Cohen and Richard L. Park, June 1978

The Kremlin and Labor: A Study in National Security Policy by Roy Godson, November 1977

The Evolution of Soviet Security Strategy, 1965-1975 by Avigdor Haselkorn, November 1977

The Geopolitics of the Nuclear Era by Colin S. Gray, September 1977

The Sino-Soviet Confrontation: Implications for the Future by Harold C. Hinton, September 1976

Food, Foreign Policy, and Raw Materials Cartels by William Schneider, February 1976

Strategic Weapons: An Introduction by Norman Polmar, October 1975

Soviet Sources of Military Doctrine and Strategy by William F. Scott, July 1975

Detente: Promises and Pitfalls by Gerald L. Steibel, March 1975 (Out of print)

Oil, Politics, and Sea Power: The Indian Ocean Vortex by Ian W.A.C. Adie, December 1974

The Soviet Presence in Latin America by James D. Theberge, June 1974

The Horn of Africa by J. Bowyer Bell, Jr., December 1973

Research and Development and the Prospects for International Security by Frederick Seitz and Rodney W. Nichols, December 1973

Raw Material Supply in a Multipolar World by Yuan-li Wu, October 1973 (Out of print)

The People's Liberation Army: Communist China's Armed Forces by Angus M. Fraser, August 1973 (Out of print)

Nuclear Weapons and the Atlantic Alliance by Wynfred Joshua, May 1973

How to Think About Arms Control and Disarmament by James E. Dougherty, May 1973 (Out of print)

National Strategy Information Center, Inc.

The Military Indoctrination of Soviet Youth by Leon Goure, January 1973 (Out of print)

The Asian Alliance: Japan and United States Policy by Franz Michael and Gaston J. Sigur, October 1972 (Out of print)

Iran, the Arabian Peninsula, and the Indian Ocean by R. M. Burrell and Alvin J. Cottrell, September 1972 (Out of print)

Soviet Naval Power: Challenge for the 1970s by Norman Polmar, April 1972. Revised edition, September 1974 (Out of print)

How Can We Negotiate with the Communists? by Gerald L. Steibel, March 1972 (Out of print)

Soviet Political Warfare Techniques, Espionage and Propaganda in the 1970s by Lyman B. Kirkpatrick, Jr., and Howland H. Sargeant, January 1972 (Out of print)

The Soviet Presence in the Eastern Mediterranean by Lawrence L. Whetten, September 1971 (Out of print)

*The Military Unbalance
Is the U.S. Becoming a Second Class power?* June 1971 (Out of print)

The Future of South Vietnam by Brigadier F. P. Serong, February 1971 (Out of print)

Strategy and National Interests: Reflections for the Future by Bernard Brodie, January 1971 (Out of print)

The Mekong River: A Challenge in Peaceful Development for Southeast Asia by Eugene R. Black, December 1970 (Out of print)

Problems of Strategy in the Pacific and Indian Oceans by George G. Thomson, October 1970 (Out of print)

Soviet Penetration into the Middle East by Wynfred Joshua, July 1970. Revised edition, October 1971 (Out of print)

Australian Security Policies and Problems by Justus M. van der Kroef, May 1970 (Out of print)

Detente: Dilemma or Disaster? by Gerald L. Steibel, July 1969 (Out of print)

National Strategy Information Center, Inc.

The Prudent Case for Safeguard by William R. Kintner, June 1969 (Out of print)

AGENDA PAPERS

Power Projection: A Net Assessment of U.S. and Soviet Capabilities by W. Scott Thompson, April 1978

Understanding the Soviet Military Threat, How CIA Estimates Went Astray by William T. Lee, February 1977

Toward a New Defense for NATO, The Case for Tactical Nuclear Weapons, July 1976 (Out of print)

Seven Tracks to Peace in the Middle East by Frank R. Barnett, April 1975

Arms Treaties with Moscow: Unequal Terms Unevenly Applied? by Donald G. Brennan, April 1975 (Out of print)

Toward a US Energy Policy by Klaus Knorr, March 1975 (Out of print)

Can We Avert Economic Warfare in Raw Materials? US Agriculture as a Blue Chip by William Schneider, July 1974

OTHER PUBLICATIONS

Arms, Men, and Military Budgets: Issues for Fiscal Year 1979 by Francis P. Hoeber, David B. Kassing, and William Schneider, Jr., February 1978

Arms, Men, and Military Budgets: Issues for Fiscal Year 1978 edited by Francis P. Hoeber and William Schneider, Jr., May 1977

Oil, Divestiture and National Security edited by Frank N. Trager, December 1976

Alternatives to Detente by Frank R. Barnett, July 1976

Arms, Men, and Military Budgets: Issues for Fiscal Year 1977 edited by William Schneider, Jr., and Francis P. Hoeber, May 1976

Indian Ocean Naval Limitations, Regional Issues and Global Implications by Alvin J. Cottrell and Walter F. Hahn, April 1976